The Aerospace Industry

Two week loan

Please return on or before the last date stamped below.
Charges are made for late return.

338 · 47629 (1) A

Researched and written by Reference Services, Central Office of Information.

© Crown copyright 1993
Applications for reproduction should be made to HMSO.
First published 1993

ISBN 0 11 701727 2

HMSO publications are available from:

HMSO Publications Centre
(Mail, fax and telephone orders only)
PO Box 276, London SW8 5DT
Telephone orders 071-873 9090
General enquiries 071-873 0011
(queuing system in operation for both numbers)
Fax orders 071-873 8200

HMSO Bookshops
49 High Holborn, London WC1V 6HB   071-873 0011
Fax 071-873 8200 (counter service only)
258 Broad Street, Birmingham B1 2HE   021-643 3740   Fax 021-643 6510
Southey House, 33 Wine Street, Bristol BS1 2BQ
0272 264306   Fax 0272 294515
9-21 Princess Street, Manchester M60 8AS   061-834 7201   Fax 061-833 0634
16 Arthur Street, Belfast BT1 4GD   0232 238451   Fax 0232 235401
71 Lothian Road, Edinburgh EH3 9AZ   031-228 4181   Fax 031-229 2734

HMSO's Accredited Agents
(see Yellow Pages)

and through good booksellers

8 JAN 1998

Contents

Acknowledgments

This book has been compiled with the co-operation of the following organisations, which the Central Office of Information would like to thank for their contributions: the Department of Trade and Industry, British Aerospace, Rolls-Royce, Short Brothers and Westland Group.

Photograph Credits

Numbers refer to the pages of the illustration section (1–8): Cossor Electronics front cover (bottom right); Short Brothers front cover (top), p.1 (top), p.2 (top), p.3 (top), p.5 (top); British Aerospace p.1 (centre), p.2 (bottom), p.4 (top), p.7 (bottom); Airbus Industrie front cover (centre), p.1 (bottom); Rolls-Royce p.3 (bottom); p.4 (middle); GEC Avionics p.4 (bottom); Martin Baker Aircraft p.5 (centre); Westland Group p.5 (bottom); GEC Sensors p.6 (top); Slingsby Aviation p.6 (centre); Didsbury Engineering p.6 (bottom); British National Space Centre front cover (bottom left), p.7 (top); British Aerospace Space Systems p.8 (top); Matra Marconi Space (UK) p.8 (bottom).

Introduction

Britain's aerospace industry is the third largest in the world, after those of the United States and the Commonwealth of Independent States. It accounts for over 2 per cent of Britain's gross domestic product, some 3 per cent of manufactured products, and nearly 8 per cent of manufactured exports.

One of only three industries in the world having total aerospace capabilities, it covers the whole spectrum of aerospace— from basic research, concept, design, development and manufacture, through all stages of test to final production across the entire range of aerospace products. These include airframes, aero-engines, guided weapons and space satellites, as well as systems, sub-systems and associated services. Its products are among the most technologically advanced and expensive to produce, with some projects costing many thousands of millions of pounds to develop.

Two companies dominate the industry, British Aerospace (BAe) and Rolls-Royce, but in addition to several smaller aircraft manufacturers, there is a huge number of electronics and equipment sub-contractors supplying the prime contractors. With electronic and other equipment often making up about 40 per cent of a modern aircraft, companies such as BAe, GEC, and Westland have developed their own electronics and systems capability.

The military aerospace industry is especially strong in avionics (aviation electronics) and in the manufacture of complex components and systems. The turnover of aerospace equipment systems in recent years has risen very substantially and now rivals that of the airframe and aero-engine manufacturers. The advent of missiles and space vehicles and the development of increasingly complex electronics since the 1960s has helped transform the aircraft industry.

There is in the industry great depth in technical and management expertise. Firms can undertake prime contractor responsibilities for major projects and even act as a total procurement agency—for instance, for a complete defence infrastructure with equipment and support. The aerospace industry is an important component of Britain's defence industry, now the world's second largest supplier of defence equipment.

Britain first established its aircraft industry when the Short Brothers set up a production line on the Isle of Sheppey in 1909 to manufacture Wright Flyers under licence. It has led the world in many aspects of aerospace design, research and development during the twentieth century, producing the revolutionary hovercraft (an air-cushion vehicle); the first all-metal, stressed-skin aeroplane, the Silver Streak; the Harrier, the world's first operational vertical and short take-off and landing (V/STOL) aircraft; the ultra-quiet Rolls-Royce RB211 engine; Concorde (jointly with France); and some of the most advanced and widely used radar, navigation and communications equipment. Other pioneering achievements involving British technologists and aviation specialists include automatic landing, swing-wing military aircraft, 'fly-by-wire', 'head-up' display, flight simulators and ejection seats. British companies have also been prime contractors for a number of major European satellite projects.

Further information on developments in the aerospace industry is contained in *Current Affairs: A Monthly Survey*, published by HMSO.

Development of the Industry

Early Pioneers

The first powered flight in Britain was made at Farnborough, on 16 October 1908, some five years after the Wright Brothers' flight. Formerly the site of the Army Balloon Factory, Farnborough became the Royal Aircraft Factory in 1912 and played a major role in early British aircraft design and production. The British aircraft industry initially supported a few pioneer aviators, but the first world war (1914–18) greatly accelerated the technology and led to mass production. The war provided the stimulus which proved and refined the basic technical characteristics of the aeroplane and its lightweight piston engine.

By 1915 pressures of war led to the Royal Aircraft Factory opening up design to companies under a system of competitive tendering, and a partnership between government and industry was formed. By 1918 the industry had expanded rapidly to serve the needs of the Royal Flying Corps and Royal Navy Air Service, which were joined to form the Royal Air Force—and some 10,000 aircraft were being built annually. In 1916 a trade association, the Society of British Aircraft (now Aerospace) Companies (SBAC), was founded with 48 members. The Royal Aircraft Factory, which had been attached to the Army, became the Royal Aircraft Establishment (RAE), undertaking aeronautical research for both the armed services and industry.

The war had stimulated a number of companies, including Napier, and Rolls-Royce—which had been founded in 1906—to establish themselves as manufacturers of aero-engines. The period also saw the first steps taken by the aviation electronics industry: radio was used in aircraft for the first time in 1910, by Marconi. By 1918 the British aircraft industry was the largest and most technologically capable in the world, comprising over 120 firms employing 112,000 people and producing around 1,250 aircraft a month.

Inter-war Developments

The first world war provided the technical basis for the development of passenger-carrying aircraft, with Alcock and Brown's 1919 transatlantic flight made in a modified Vickers Vimy bomber. Firms turned to producing civil aeroplanes. Short Brothers' monoplane Empire C-class flying boats, the de Havilland Moth series, and Handley Page's HP42 biplane were early airliners, and many people gained their first experience of flight in a de Havilland light aircraft. By the early 1940s, the flying boat was superseded by the long-range land-based airliner.

During the 1920s and 1930s the growth of commercial aviation brought about innovation in structures and aerodynamics, leading to the development of the stressed metal, multi-engined monoplane.

Following a lull caused mainly by the abrupt cancellation of military orders at the end of the first world war, the Government decided by 1924 that the aircraft industry had to be maintained and civil aviation fostered. It introduced a series of measures to encourage all aspects of aviation. The Air Ministry allocated contracts to a selected group of competing companies, which tended to specialise in certain product areas, employing major design teams. For example, Gloster, Hawker and Bristol concentrated on fighter aircraft; Blackburn, Shorts and Supermarine on flying-boats; and Fairey, light bombers and seaplanes such as the IIIF and Swordfish. In

1920 Shorts produced Silver Streak, the world's first all-metal, stressed-skin aeroplane; in 1932, its Sarafand flying-boat became the largest aircraft built to date. Shorts' Sunderland flying-boat, built for the RAF in 1938, continued in service for 21 years. Although not part of this group, de Havilland had considerable commercial success with its range of light aircraft, beginning with the 1924 Moth.

The interwar industry comprised 52 companies, with the top 16 employing 90 per cent of the workforce. A series of mergers took place, including Hawker's acquisition of Armstrong-Siddeley, A. V. Roe and Gloster, to form the Hawker-Siddeley group in 1935. Britain's major airline, Imperial Airways, had been formed in 1924 following mergers of various operators, and began to operate routes to India in 1926.

During this period Rolls-Royce emerged as the most technologically advanced of the group of aero-engine companies. When government funding became available in 1924, it was able to produce the Kestrel and the 'R' series which laid the foundation for the renowned Merlin engine. Rolls-Royce's Jupiter remained Britain's most important aero-engine throughout the 1930s. The Schneider Trophy air races encouraged innovation, including development of the Merlin engine and the Spitfire fighter. British aircraft won several world records for speed, altitude and endurance during the 1920s and early 1930s. A group of forward-looking, imaginative designers launched private ventures, including early work by Supermarine and Hawker on the Spitfire and Hurricane respectively, and Vickers' 'geodetic' (lattice-structured) bomber airframe derived from Barnes Wallis's R100 airship design, which in turn led to the Wellington bomber.

In the 1920s exports accounted for 20 per cent of airframe, and 40 per cent of engine, output. In 1934 the drive for parity with the

German air force marked the beginning of rearmament, and the home market began to absorb the bulk of production. As a result, the industry expanded rapidly. In 1936 the Air Ministry implemented a 'shadow factory' scheme, which entailed commissioning other suitable manufacturing companies, such as those in the motor vehicle industry, to produce airframes and engines. Additional factories and plant were financed by the Government. The Nuffield (Morris) organisation was to manage the largest aircraft factory in Europe, producing 70 per cent of all Spitfires built during the second world war (1939–45). Several firms benefited from the new plant, which was to be used in the post-war expansion of the industry. The Rolls-Royce sub-contractor system was adopted as a model for the rest of the aircraft industry.

Radar

In 1922 Marconi envisaged the use of radio waves to detect objects in darkness or fog, and this led, in 1933, to the establishment in Britain of a government-sponsored programme to develop radar. Early forms of radar made a decisive contribution to air defence during the second world war. Radar equipment and techniques were greatly extended and improved. Rapid developments were also made in airborne radio communications. The equipment put into service by the end of the war included a comprehensive ground radar system, air interception equipment for fighter aircraft, and radio navigation and positional aids for both airborne and marine use. The companies involved in their production were Marconi, Cossor and Metropolitan Vickers.

Second World War

British-made aircraft that played an outstanding role during the second world war included the Spitfire and Hurricane fighters, the four-engined Lancaster bomber, the twin-engined Mosquito and Wellington, and the Sunderland flying-boat. Over 166,000 Rolls-Royce Merlin engines were built, more than any other engine in aviation history. By 1944 Britain's aircraft and associated engineering industries were employing 1.8 million workers.

Aircraft design and manufacturing were changing from a reliance on intuitive design to a more systematic approach. During the second world war, the size and power of combat aircraft, and the range and payload of bombers, grew substantially. The speed of conventionally powered fighters such as the Spitfire rose by over 160 km/h (100 mph). The development of airborne radar, navigation aids and other advanced equipment increased the complexity of aircraft production. Specialist companies were set up to develop and produce large sub-systems which had previously been built by a main contractor. Rolls and Bristol Engines formed Rotol, a jointly owned company created to develop and manufacture propellers.

Jet Engines

The most important innovation to emerge from the second world war, the conception and creation of the first practicable jet engine—an internal combustion engine in which exhaust gases propel the aircraft after expanding through a turbine driving the compressor—was designed and built by Sir Frank Whittle in 1937. His idea for a single-stage axial-flow turbine coupled with the centrifugal compressor would become the basis of British jet development. In the early years it also anticipated the development of materials capable of withstanding high stresses and temperatures. Another engine designed by Whittle powered the first British jet flight, by the Gloster E28/39, in 1941.

The jet was the driving force behind a new generation of civil and military aircraft of greatly increased size, power and range. In

1946 Rolls-Royce was the first company to abandon piston technology entirely. Rolls took over a Rover factory to pursue development of the jet, which required new manufacturing techniques. It also took over Sir Frank Whittle's company, Power Jets. Production lines were established in 1946 at Rolls's Derby plant. In 1943 research began on high-speed aerodynamics and structures which led to the development of a high-speed interceptor aircraft.

The first production model of a British jet-powered aeroplane, the Gloster Meteor, flew in 1944 and was used successfully to intercept V1 flying bombs. Rolls-Royce turned the Whittle design into the Derwent series in 1945. The world's first turboprop aircraft (the pure jet engine driving a propeller) was a test version of the Meteor and flew that same year.

Brabazon Report

During the war the aircraft industry had emerged as a major manufacturing sector of strategic importance. Although military aviation would dominate it for some time, the Government intended that commercial aircraft should form a significant part of post-war plans for expansion. Most of the research carried out on new equipment came from the Royal Aircraft Establishment and other government research bodies, with firms such as Bristol and de Havilland starting to build up their own research capabilities.

A wartime government committee headed by Lord Brabazon recommended nine airliner projects (see Table 1) which formed the basis of Britain's post-war civil aircraft industry. One project involved turbojet flights carrying mail and passengers throughout the British Commonwealth. The turbojet was the de Havilland Comet 1, for which the company used the Whittle centrifugal compressor concept.

Table 1: Brabazon Types

Type of Aircraft	Description
Type 1 Bristol Brabazon	Long-range piston-engined transatlantic airliner
Type 2A Airspeed Ambassador	Short-range piston-engined airliner
Type 2B Vickers Viscount	Short-range turboprop airliner
Type 2B Armstrong-Whitworth Apollo	Short-range turboprop airliner
Type 3A Avro 693	Medium-range turboprop airliner
Type 3B Avro Tudor II	Developed from interim aircraft (replaced Avro 693)
Type 4 de Havilland Comet	Originally designed as transatlantic 'mail carrier'
Type 5A Miles Marathon	Piston-engined feederliner
Type 5B de Havilland Dove	Piston-engined feederliner

Output

By 1945 over 126,500 aircraft had been delivered. In 1935 the industry employed some 35,000 people and had an output worth £14 million. By 1944 output was valued at £800 million and the aircraft companies alone employed 300,000 workers. Aircraft production had spawned a new light metal industry in Britain. In terms of scale, speed and cost, the development of the aircraft industry had no parallel.

Post-war Developments

In the post-war years, technological competition hastened the pace of innovation. Immediately following the war, production techniques were modernised and worn-out machinery replaced. All piston-engined combat aircraft had to be refitted with jets. Despite the fall in demand for military aircraft, the Brabazon programme and the export of both civil and military aircraft helped to maintain a broadly based industry. The two national airlines were British Overseas Airways Corporation (BOAC), formed in 1939 from a merger of Imperial Airways and British Airways, and British European Airways (BEA), set up in 1946 to operate domestic and European services.

De Havilland had three major aircraft programmes—the Comet civil jet airliner, Vampire jet fighter, and Dove and Heron, which were a continuation of de Havilland's series of small airliners.

From about 1948 onwards, manufacturers concentrated on developing gas-turbine-powered civil aircraft. In 1952 the de Havilland Comet became the first commercial jet aircraft to enter passenger service. It was also the first airliner to have fully powered flight controls. Later that year BOAC began a weekly Comet service from London to Sri Lanka (then Ceylon), which cut travel time from around 34 hours to just over 21 hours.

In 1958 a BOAC Comet 4 began the world's first passenger jet transatlantic service. The first Comet series could carry 36 passengers at an average speed of 780 km/h (490 mph)—around 270 km/h (167 mph) faster than a piston-driven aircraft. The airliner was later modified for RAF service. The Comet 4 continued as a commercial airliner, fitted with Rolls-Royce Avon engines, until the United States Boeing 707 overtook its sales. The Comet airframe is still in service with the RAF as the Nimrod ASW.

Vickers and Bristol became specialists in civil aircraft while maintaining an important fighter aircraft design capability. Handley Page maintained both civil and military programmes.

With the end of flying-boat production in 1947 Shorts, already based in Belfast, closed its remaining English factory and became Short Brothers and Harland of Northern Ireland. Its SC1, the world's first fixed-wing vertical take-off and landing aircraft, made its maiden flight in 1957. English Electric, one of the main wartime producers, assembled the Vampire jet fighter and opened the first privately owned supersonic wind tunnel in Britain and possibly the first outside the United States. It also pioneered the use of computers in design and development. The company became noted for several important post-war military aircraft, including the Canberra jet bomber and Britain's first operational supersonic fighter, the P1 Lightning.

In the early post-war period, piston-engined commercial aircraft were manufactured on a large scale. British aero-engines achieved a worldwide reputation during this period. Of Britain's eight aero-engine companies developing new turbine engines under government contract, Rolls-Royce engines, such as the Nene and Tay military engines, proved commercially the most successful. Along with Armstrong-Siddeley and Bristol, Rolls began developing axial-flow jets with increased engine thrust and improved fuel consumption.

By the mid-1950s Rolls-Royce engines powered most of the Royal Air Force's front line aircraft and formed the basis for a range of civil designs. The Vickers Viscount was the world's first propeller turbine-powered airliner to enter service, in 1953, and has been in service for 40 years. Some 440 Viscounts were sold overseas, including to the United States. The Viscount's Rolls-Royce Dart engine was in production until 1986. Rolls-Royce introduced the world's first ever turbofan engine, the Conway, in the 1950s; this powered versions of the Boeing 707 and DC 8. Now the most common derivative of the gas turbine for aircraft propulsion,

the turbofan is a 'bypass' engine which gives better propulsive efficiency at lower aircraft speeds, lower noise levels and improved fuel
consumption. After a temporary reduction in military aircraft
orders in the mid-1950s, sales rose steadily through the late 1950s;
the larger sellers included the Canberra, the Lightning, the V-
bombers, the Hunter and Javelin. In the same period several airframe and electronics firms became involved in guided weapons
programmes.

Rediffusion Simulation built the first fully electronic flight
simulator in Europe in 1950.

Company Mergers
In the mid-1950s there were 31 full members of the SBAC. The six
biggest companies, Vickers, English Electric, Hawker-Siddeley
(the largest), Rolls-Royce, Bristol and de Havilland accounted for
around 80 per cent of production. As aircraft became more complex and expensive to produce, it was necessary for companies to
achieve production levels that would generate economies of scale.
At the end of the 1950s a series of company mergers resulted in the
creation of three main airframe and two engine groups (see diagram
on p. 13).

Vickers and English Electric merged to form the British
Aircraft Corporation (BAC). BAC produced a medium-range air-
liner, the BAC One-Eleven, as well as inheriting the VC10, TSR2,
Lightning, and various guided weapons projects. Hawker-Siddeley
took over de Havilland and others to form Hawker-Siddeley
Aviation (HSA). Helicopter production was centred on a single
firm, Westland. Among companies unaffected by the mergers were
Shorts, which developed a substantial missile production capacity,
and Rolls-Royce. The other aero-engine company, Bristol-
Siddeley Engines (BSE), was formed in 1959 as a result of a merger
between Bristol Aero-Engines and Armstrong-Siddeley Motors.

The British Aircraft Industry, 1960

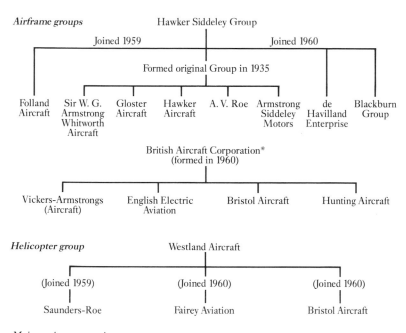

Airframe groups

Hawker Siddeley Group

Joined 1959 — Joined 1960

Formed original Group in 1935

Folland Aircraft · Sir W. G. Armstrong Whitworth Aircraft · Gloster Aircraft · Hawker Aircraft · A. V. Roe · Armstrong Siddeley Motors · de Havilland Enterprise · Blackburn Group

British Aircraft Corporation*
(formed in 1960)

Vickers-Armstrongs (Aircraft) · English Electric Aviation · Bristol Aircraft · Hunting Aircraft

Helicopter group

Westland Aircraft

(Joined 1959) · (Joined 1960) · (Joined 1960)

Saunders-Roe · Fairey Aviation · Bristol Aircraft

Main engine companies

1 Bristol Siddeley – formed in 1959 by merger on 50:50 basis of Bristol Aero-Engines and Armstrong Siddeley Motors
2 Rolls-Royce

*BAC and the Hawker Siddeley Group were merged and nationalised as British Aerospace in 1977 and formed as a public limited company in 1981.

The 1960s

The 1960s witnessed the introduction of British-built airliners such as the VC10, BAC One-Eleven, Trident and HS 748, the SD 330 regional aircraft, and also the operation of turbofan engines.

Output

By the end of the 1960s, the aerospace industry contributed around 3 per cent of Britain's manufacturing output. Rolls-Royce took over Bristol-Siddeley Engines in the mid-1960s, which together made up 64 per cent. Between 1961 and 1967, exports averaged around one-fifth of the industry's total output, with engines making up 43 per cent of overseas sales (excluding engines in British airframe exports). The industry employed some 247,000 people.

The Labour Government of the early 1960s encouraged the creation of larger industrial groupings—'national champions'—to improve their competitiveness at home and abroad. A fundamental review of the industry, the Plowden Report, assessed the potential of international co-operation to offset rising development costs of large projects.

Concorde

Extensive development work in the 1960s and early 1970s resulted in the building of the Anglo-French Concorde, the world's first supersonic passenger aircraft. Some 60 per cent of the engine design was carried out in Britain. The first commercial supersonic jet service began in January 1976. International collaboration would bring long-term commitment to programmes and stability to the industry, and Concorde paved the way for future joint programmes.

The aircraft carries 100 passengers at speeds around Mach 2 (2,170 km/h) over journeys of 5,630 km (3,500 miles), cutting journey times by about one-half. One of the most advanced aircraft the European industry has ever produced, Concorde combines military power and performance with a commercial airliner's reliability and safety. Although only 16 out of an originally intended 400 aircraft were built, Concorde became profitable in the 1980s and continues to attract a steady supply of charter business as well as being used on scheduled flights. British Aerospace is one of several companies studying the feasibility of developing a successor to Concorde.

Other Collaborative Programmes

Further civil and military projects undertaken by Britain and France included the Jaguar attack/trainer combat aircraft, the Puma, Lynx and Gazelle helicopters, the Martel missile, and a wide-bodied medium-range airliner, Airbus. In 1968 Britain, Germany and Italy agreed to build a multi-role combat aircraft, which was to become the Tornado. The Tornado project was, at the time, at the forefront of technology. Rolls-Royce and Turboméca of France joined forces to develop the Adour turbofan engine to power the Jaguar and, later, the British Aerospace Hawk and McDonnell Douglas Goshawk.

In the 1960s initial plans were also laid for the development of a 225–250-seat twin-engined airliner, the short- and medium-range A300 Airbus.

Technological Advances

Earlier work on vertical or short take-off and landing (V/STOL) prototypes led to the entry into service in 1969 of the Harrier 'jump-jet' by Hawker-Siddeley Aviation, which is still the only fully operational V/STOL aircraft. During the 1950s Rolls-Royce had supplied engines for over half the Western world's jet airliners.

The 1960s saw rapid developments in electronic equipment. The industry pioneered the use of computers in design and manufacturing processes. During this period 30 per cent of digital computers in Britain were used for aerospace work. Other significant advances included the introduction of Doppler navigation systems (see p. 76); automatic direction finders and direction-measuring equipment; the advent of miniaturised airborne navigation computers; weapons-firing systems and data processing; and the pioneering of autopilots and airborne instrument landing systems (see p. 86). In the late 1950s a British partnership headed by Smiths Industries produced the first automatic landing system to be certificated for passenger-carrying service. The first ever automatic landing on a scheduled airline flight was made by a British European Airways Trident in 1967.

Since the early 1960s a range of national and international space activities has been undertaken in Britain. Satellites, sounding rockets and ground stations have been constructed for national agencies by the aerospace industry, which has also played a role in European space programmes. Britain helped to set up the European Space Agency (ESA) in the 1970s.

The 1970s Onwards

Greatly increased costs of developing the RB211 for Lockheed led to Rolls-Royce being taken over by the Government in 1971, continuing as a private-sector company but with the Government as single shareholder. A renegotiated contract with Lockheed provided the foundation for Rolls-Royce's new generation of RB211 engines.

Major increases in oil prices during the 1970s, coupled with greater competition between airlines, helped transform the aerospace industry, with engine and airframe manufacturers concentrating more than ever on improving fuel economy. This has been achieved by using lighter materials such as titanium and carbon-fibre composites, together with better aerodynamic techniques. Rolls-Royce attained major fuel savings through advanced engine designs and, like other leading engine manufacturers, has developed much quieter engines in response to stricter noise standards.

In 1975 the industry's exports amounted to £800 million. By 1988 total orders stood at around £20,000 million. In the 1960s Britain's share of world aerospace markets was 10 per cent; by the mid-1970s it was 14 per cent, and in the 1980s nearly 17 per cent. In 1988 aerospace companies employed some 200,000 people, producing £9,000 million in total turnover. In 1987 the industry exported over 60 per cent of turnover, with a record trade balance of £2,400 million. In the years since 1977 aerospace has never had a negative trade balance.

British Aerospace

As the aerospace industry's largest customer and source of launch capital for civil projects, the Government played a major role in determining the industry's strategy and workload. BAC, HSA, Hawker-Siddeley Dynamics and Scottish Aviation were merged and nationalised as British Aerospace (BAe) in 1977, remaining in public hands for four years.

The formation of BAe completed the rationalisation process begun in the 1950s. It created one of the strongest aerospace companies in Europe with some 70,000 employees, net assets of over £300 million and an annual turnover of £700 million.

International collaboration became established as the basis for major airframe projects, and most military engine developments, in order to compete more successfully with the major United States manufacturers. In the early 1970s HSA remained a major sub-contractor to Airbus Industrie after the Government withdrew from Airbus, with responsibility for developing and manufacturing Airbus wings. BAe joined Airbus as a full partner in 1979, since when it has assumed a major role in further Airbus projects, including the highly successful A320. Development began in 1978 on the BAe 146, which entered service in 1983. At less than 86 decibels on take-off and landing, the BAe 146 is considered to be one of the world's quietest jet airliners.

Rolls-Royce

Rolls-Royce developed the RB211, the first of a generation of engines for a large number of airliners, having received £250 million in launch aid from the Government. The RB211 series included: the -22B for the Lockheed LO11 Tristar; the -524 for the long-range L1011; the -524 for the Boeing 747 and the -535C for the Boeing B757. By 1978 the series offered engines ranging from 40,000 lb to around 70,000 lb of thrust.

In the mid-1980s Rolls-Royce developed the 12-15,000-lb Tay engine. In 1988 the largest RB211 engine, the -524G, later renamed the Trent, was launched for the bigger Boeing 747s.

Rolls-Royce was returned to private ownership in 1987. Its sales and profits grew substantially during the 1980s, with 70 per cent of total output exported. The company also introduced various cost-saving measures, such as automated production, including robotics. Currently in production are engines for the 747, 757 and 767 Boeing airliners, with the Trent under development for the 777.

In collaboration with other European companies, Rolls-Royce produces engines for the Tornado and is developing the engine for the European Fighter Aircraft (see p. 70).

Recent Technological Advances

The biggest passenger- and car-carrying hovercraft in the world is the Super 4, which came into service in the late 1970s. In 1982 the British Hovercraft Corporation produced the first diesel-engined welded-aluminium hovercraft, the SRN4. By 1990 SRN4 hovercraft had carried more than 33 million people and 4.6 million cars across the English Channel.

Based on research carried out at the Royal Aircraft Establishment in the 1970s, British Aerospace, with Marconi and Dowty Boulton Paul, developed a system in the 1980s of moving flying control surfaces by electronic rather than mechanical means. 'Fly-by-wire', as it is known (see pp. 86-9), is incorporated in the Airbus series. GEC Avionics also developed and flew the world's first fly-by-light system; this optically signalled system was first used in 1988 in an airship.

The concept of head-up display (HUD), which electronically projects symbols into the pilot's view, thus avoiding the need to look down at cockpit instruments, was pioneered and developed by the Royal Aerospace Establishment (then the Royal Aircraft Establishment). GEC Avionics is the world's major manufacturer of high-brightness HUDs. The company has also developed a holographic HUD, which enables pilots to fly at high speeds at very low altitude in the dark.

Martin-Baker Aircraft, pioneers of aircraft ejection seats since the second world war, constructed the world's first microprocessor-controlled ejection seat in 1984.

The Industry Today

The British aerospace industry is now a major, world-class manufacturing sector made up of almost 300 companies, including 250
member companies of the SBAC, employing over 170,000 people.
In 1991 it had a turnover of around £10,500 million. Overseas sales,
valued at almost £8,000 million in 1991, accounted for around 12
per cent of world aerospace exports, through direct sales and in collaborative ventures with overseas firms. The balance of trade in
1991 was about £2,500 million.

Britain's aerospace equipment industry is Europe's largest.
The United States is the industry's biggest export customer, taking
around a quarter of total exports. With the global reduction in
defence spending following the ending of the Cold War, spending
on civil products is now about the same as that for defence
products.

The emergence of electronics and systems integration has led
to greater diversification in the industry. Increasing complexity of
programmes has fostered a very high level of managerial skills.
Since the end of 1990 the total workforce has been reduced by
over 25,000. However, the industry has substantially improved
productivity.

The industry's biggest customer is the Ministry of Defence.
The British air transport industry takes only a small proportion of
the aerospace industry's output, although many airliners bought
from United States companies such as Boeing are fitted with
British-made engines and other equipment. In addition to manufacturing their own aircraft and helicopters, the larger firms, such

as British Aerospace, Shorts and Westland, supply components to each other and to the other major aircraft and aero-engine manufacturers in Britain and overseas. Smaller and medium-size firms are heavily dependent on orders from large companies at home and abroad.

Range of the Industry

Major Companies

British Aerospace is Britain's largest producer of civil and military aircraft, with factories across the country. The company also makes satellites, space systems, guided weapons and components. Following the 1977 merger (see p. 17), British Aerospace was formed as a public limited company in 1981 and fully privatised in 1985, with the aim of increasing competitiveness within the international aerospace industry. The merger made BAe Britain's seventh and Europe's twenty-fourth largest.

BAe has diversified its operations in high technology and manufacturing. It has expanded its systems and electronics activities, improving its in-house software and systems design capability. It is now a major producer of gyroscopes (used to control and stabilise the course of aircraft and missiles), navigation equipment, and custom-designed micro-circuitry. Its aircraft cover the entire technological spectrum from V/STOL and swing-wing combat aircraft to wide-body and turboprop airliners, and from basic to advanced jet trainers. Since 1978 BAe and its partners have delivered thousands of aircraft to customers in more than 50 countries.

The bulk of BAe's profits, like most aerospace companies, is derived from military activities. In the face of declining defence orders and a global recession affecting the world civil aviation industries, the company has unified its defence operations and restructured commercial aircraft activities into three separate units for regional aircraft, Airbus and corporate jets.

Rolls-Royce is one of the Western world's three leading manufacturers of aero-engines. The company, which was returned to private ownership in 1987, designs, develops and manufactures gas-turbine engines for aircraft, helicopters and industrial and marine purposes. Its main factories are in Bristol, Derby, Coventry, Barnoldswick and East Kilbride. It also has extensive power engineering interests following a merger with NEI.

Westland Group is a leading aerospace company with an annual turnover of £400 million and some 9,000 employees. It has a broad technological capability in all its companies and is a participant in key international collaborative programmes. Westland Group companies are involved in major civil and military projects, such as the Anglo-Italian EH101 advanced medium-lift helicopter and the development of airliners in North America and Europe.

Established since the beginning of aviation, Short Brothers of Belfast was privatised in 1989 after 46 years of state ownership. It is now part of the European Group of Bombardier Inc of Canada. The company manufactures civil and military aircraft, aircraft components, and is a world leader in close air defence missile systems. It is a major world supplier of nacelle systems (outer engine casings) and components, having made substantial design contributions to their development, notably in the areas of noise attenuation and the use of advanced, lightweight composites.

Several companies are engaged in the manufacture of light aircraft. These include Lovaux and Slingsby Aviation. Slingsby, which also makes airships and hovercraft, made its reputation by supplying gliders to the RAF and others. Other companies, such as Brooklands Aerospace, Island Aircraft, Norman Aeroplane and

Pilatus Britten-Norman, make observation, two-seater, agricultural, all-purpose utility and glider aircraft.

Aerospace Equipment Industry

Numerous other companies supply components, sub-assemblies and spares, and these make a significant contribution to the industry's technological standing and to its sales. Some 100 British equipment manufacturers supply systems and equipment to the Airbus programme alone. Major companies include Lucas Aerospace, Dowty (now merged with Tube Investments), Dunlop, Vickers Precision Instruments, Fairey Hydraulics and Normalair-Garrett (NGL). Lucas Aerospace is a world leader in the specialist field of fuel pump technology. Its products include axial piston, radial piston and turbine-driven centrifugal designs. Lucas is also a leading supplier of ignition systems and small gas-turbine engines. Digital Electronic makes engine fuel systems.

Dowty specialises in the design, development and manufacture of gas-turbine engine controls and accessories, including digital electronic controls, limiters, pumps, flow controls, metering valves and actuation control for all Rolls-Royce Pegasus-powered Harrier aircraft. Normalair-Garrett has designed and produced high-speed turbo machinery for aircraft since the early 1950s. It makes power plants for use in unmanned aircraft.

Dowty Rotol has manufactured propellers since 1937 and is currently producing high-technology units for general aviation, commuter and turboprop airliners. Vickers Precision Instruments is a leading precision component manufacturer specialising in investment casting, machining, fabrication and repair of engine-run components, and sheet metal components in super alloys and stainless steel. Fairey Hydraulics manufactures control systems for aircraft, landing gear and other equipment, and guided weapons.

The avionics industry, having pioneered many major technical advances in airborne communications systems, produces world class equipment for civil and military purposes. Many of the firms in this area are the subsidiaries of large corporate groups. They include GEC Avionics, GEC Sensors, GEC-Plessey Avionics, Ferranti, the Marconi Group, Lucas Aerospace, Cossor Electronics, Racal, Smiths Industries and THORN EMI. GEC Sensors pioneered the use of radio in aircraft, and GEC-Plessey designed the world's first UHF/VHF transceiver (which incorporates circuitry used for reception or transmission). Rediffusion Simulation, Link-Miles and British Aerospace are among the world's leading companies in the production of simulation equipment for training.

International Partnerships

Since the 1960s, collaborative development of civil and military aircraft has become ever more important because of the substantial capital sums needed to launch development and production programmes. A long-established reputation for innovation and technical excellence, and a proven ability to manage sophisticated, complex aerospace projects have resulted in the British industry being a collaborator in many international aerospace programmes. These include several major projects linking European aerospace manufacturers, like the Airbus series of airliners, the Fokker 100 passenger aircraft, the Tornado and European Fighter Aircraft, helicopters such as the EH101, missiles, aero-engines and space activities.

British Aerospace has had a long association with McDonnell Douglas in the United States in the design of the Harrier II and Goshawk military aircraft. Work on the Swedish JAS 39 Gripen

fighter involved BAe and Saab. The Tornado is built by a trina-
tional consortium made up of BAe, MBB of Germany and Alenia
of Italy. BAe is one of the partner companies in Eurofighter, a four-
nation consortium presently involving firms from Britain,
Germany, Italy and Spain in the development of the European
Fighter Aircraft.

Around 30 per cent of Britain's aerospace equipment industry
turnover is collaborative. Some 250 British aerospace and avionics
companies are currently active in partnership with overseas companies. British companies are also discussing collaboration with partners in the Commonwealth of Independent States (CIS). The
Tupolev Tu204 flew at the 1992 Farnborough Air Show with
Rolls-Royce RB211-535 engines.

Dowty and Lucas Aerospace have maintained licence agreements and joint ventures with overseas companies for over 40
years. The Jaguar programme with France led Dowty into collaboration with the same company on the Airbus programme. Its collaboration over engine controls with the People's Republic of
China has led to further development on electronic engine controls
to update China's Soviet-built aero-engines. THORN EMI
Electronics participates in some 20 collaborative projects, including a NATO anti-tank missile project with British Aerospace
Defence, Westland Helicopters and Hughes Aircraft of the United
States.

Many British companies have collaborated in space projects in
the United States and Japan, as well as with the European Space
Agency. The funding and provision of a European Transonic Wind
Tunnel, to be used by European aerospace industries and research
and development establishments, has been agreed by the governments of Britain, Germany, France and The Netherlands.

Research and Development

A significant proportion of Britain's investment in industrial research and development (R & D) is devoted to the aerospace and aerospace electronics industries. Further funds have gone into the development of advanced materials for aerospace projects. Although government funding has amounted to well over half of total aerospace R & D, a greatly increased proportion of research funds is now being provided by private companies. Total expenditure on aerospace R & D in 1990 was £918 million—17 per cent of R & D undertaken in manufacturing as a whole. Some 22,000 people are employed on aerospace R & D.

Most developmental work is carried out by industry, with some assistance from government research establishments. A substantial amount of long-term aerospace research and formal trials work is conducted in partnership with universities and industrial research centres. The Science and Engineering Research Council (SERC) also supports long-term R & D, usually within higher education institutions.

Companies such as British Aerospace, Rolls-Royce and Westland retain a fully independent civil design and development capability. Consortia are often set up by industry to establish collaboration on research between partner organisations operating in Britain and overseas. Civil aviation research relating to operations and safety is reviewed by the Civil Aviation Research and Development Board, which is adminstered by the Civil Aviation Authority (CAA).

Civil aircraft research and demonstration work is supported by the DTI's Civil Aircraft Research and Demonstration (CARAD) programme, which aims to help the aerospace industry maintain the technological base needed to compete effectively in world markets. The programme, with annual funds of around £20 million, covers pre-competitive research on airframe technology, avionics and propulsion systems related to civil aircraft, but excludes support for product development.

The bulk of the Government's spending on R & D in aerospace is concerned with military programmes and supported by the Ministry of Defence (MoD). Much of this research has civil spin-off value. A large proportion of the CARAD expenditure is devoted to funding of work carried out at the Defence Research Agency (DRA) or on the DRA's behalf at higher education institutions and in industry.

The rest of the CARAD budget funds collaborative research at higher education institutions and in industry. Only in exceptional circumstances is support given to non-collaborative projects.

Royal Aerospace Establishment

The Royal Aerospace Establishment (RAE), formerly the Royal Aircraft Establishment, is the largest R & D establishment in Europe. Now part of the DRA at Farnborough, it is the main focus for work on aircraft, guided weapons and space technology, and gas turbines. In addition to developing new products and operational techniques, it encourages industry to apply them to new aircraft and defence projects.

The DRA also incorporates the former Royal Signals and Radar Establishment, the Admiralty Research Establishment and the Royal Armaments Research and Development Establishment. It is a leading centre of, among other things, aerodynamics, communications, electronics and avionics, aerospace materials, navigation and sensors. Its facilities include large wind tunnels, simulators, and a fleet of aircraft which are used as flying test-beds for aerial experimentation. The Aeroplane and Armament

Experimental Establishment is the MoD's testing centre for all military aircraft and associated equipment destined for use in the armed services. It works in close association with industry and other test centres overseas, which is of particular benefit for collaborative projects.

Society of British Aerospace Companies

The industry's main representative body is the Society of British Aerospace Companies, which hosts the biennial Farnborough Air Show. This is regarded as one of the world's most comprehensive exhibitions for buyers of aircraft and aerospace products; some 800 companies from 30 countries were represented at the most recent show in 1992.

The 250 British companies engaged in aerospace manufacture and in aerospace/aviation repair and overhaul services are members of the SBAC. Internationally recognised as the representative body of the industry, it provides a forum for the exchange of ideas and the formulation of policy within the industry. Government looks to the SBAC for consultation on all aerospace matters.

Civil Aircraft

The principal producers of larger-scale commercial aircraft are British Aerospace and Shorts, while there are several companies engaged in developing and manufacturing smaller aircraft. The combination of the recent recession, the short-term effect of the Gulf War on passenger traffic, and increased competition, has created difficult conditions for this sector of the industry. These have resulted in further rationalisation to improve competitiveness and a greater emphasis on collaboration.

Airbus

British Aerospace holds a 20 per cent share in the European consortium Airbus Industrie, which produces the Airbus family of jet airliners. BAe is responsible for the design and manufacture of wings and fuel systems for all Airbus models, and for the fuselage system on the A321. Airbus was originally conceived in the 1960s by France, Germany and Britain to compete against the dominance of United States civil aerospace manufacturers. Members of the consortium act as both shareholders and sub-contractors, providing parts for the complete aircraft and sharing in the proceeds from sales.

Airbus projects are partly funded by the partner companies' national governments, which receive repayment in the form of levies on aircraft sales. As a result of a bilateral agreement in 1992 between the European Commission and the United States, a limit has been set on government subsidies for all new civil airliners with over 100 seats. Support granted to Airbus and other projects before the agreement was made will not be affected. British Aerospace has received launch aid on the A320 and A330/A340 projects only, which is repayable in full, with interest.

In 20 years Airbus Industrie has created a series of six technologically advanced aircraft, from 150 seats up to 400 (see Table 2). Since the A300 flew in 1972 the series has been extended to include the 220-seat A310, the 150-seat A320, the 186-seat A321, the 335-seat A330 and the ultra long-range 260-295-seat A340. The A330 and A340 are being developed in tandem with shared structures and systems. The original A300 is still in production in updated form as the 267-seat A300-600. In Britain alone, over 300 companies are involved in the production of sub-contracted items for Airbus, ranging from electronic sensors to cabin seats and furnishings. By the end of 1991 firm orders stood at over 1,830,

Table 2: Airbus Aircraft

Aircraft	Typical seating (2-class)	Thrust range (lb)
A300	251	50–53,000
A300–600	267	56–61,500
A310	218	56–59,000
A320		
A320–100	150	25,000
A321–100	150	29–30,000
A330/A340		
A330–300	335	64–68,000
A340–200	262	31,200
A340–300	295	31,200
A340–300C	230	31,200

of which 927 aircraft were in service around the world. In 1991 orders for Airbus airliners totalled 101, and some 163 were delivered to customers. The Department of Trade and Industry has contributed launch aid amounting to £250 million towards the cost of developing the A320 wing and will make up to £450 million available for the A330/A340 wing.

Six types are currently in production: the A300-600, A310, A320, A321, A330 and A340.

Airbus Family

Originally intended as a short-haul 'air bus' carrying some 250 passengers, the first A300 aircraft entered service in 1974. In 1978 Airbus Industrie launched the A310. Designed to carry fewer passengers over longer distances than the A300, it incorporated a new wing and cockpit design. By adding the later advanced technology of the A310, the A300 was developed into the A300-600 series, with increased engine power, capacity and range.

The A310 and A300–600 medium- to long-range airliners, of which a total of 600 have been delivered, have an excellent reputation for operational reliability.

The short- to medium-haul A320 was the first airliner (apart from Concorde) to be fitted with 'fly-by-wire' controls, which enable the pilot to operate within safe flying limits by preventing the aircraft from overspeeding or stalling. Since its launch in 1984 the A320 has proved the fastest-selling jet airliner to date; over 700 have been ordered and more than 330 delivered.

Three more Airbus projects are being developed. The 186-seat A321 is due to enter service in 1994, with 140 sales confirmed. The A340, the first Airbus to be powered by four engines, is designed for non-stop journeys of 7,500 nautical miles on 'long thin' routes, which are less profitable for bigger aircraft. Now in its flight test programme, the four-engined A340 is due for delivery in 1993. At almost 30 m (100 ft), the wings for the A340 are nearly twice as long as those built for the A320. Orders and options for the A340 stand at around 500.

The A340's twin-engined, sister aircraft, the A330, is due to enter service in 1994. The A330 and A340 have the same wing design, as well as a common flight deck, fuselage, nose, and main landing gear and tail unit. Firm orders for the A330 stand at 143.

BAe's Chester and Filton factories produced 50 wide-body wing sets in 1991 for the A300 and A310, together with more than 120 for the A320. Airbus Industrie is supplying United Airlines, hitherto an exclusive user of Boeing twinjets, with up to 100 medium-size A320 jetliners—50 on lease and an option for a further 50. Deliveries are due in November 1993.

A 130-seat derivative of the A320, the A319, is being marketed to airlines and will be launched if demand justifies it.

BAe 146 and Regional Jetliner

The four-engined BAe 146 has been British Aerospace's most significant 'national' civil project. Since it entered service in 1983, the 146 has attracted 212 orders, more than half for passenger versions coming from US domestic airlines.

Considered to be one of the quietest jet airliners in the world, the 146 was designed to fly from short runways in remote locations and from city centre airports. The 146's other key features are low operating costs, high fuel efficiency, ease of maintenance and operational versatility; its low noise signature has made it acceptable to very noise-sensitive areas where conventional airliners are banned. Designed particularly for developing countries, where airfield conditions can be difficult, the 146 has proved to be extremely flexible in its various roles. Variants were the QT (Quiet Trader) freight transport, the QC (Quick Change) part freight/part passenger version, and a military transport variant.

In June 1992 BAe announced the launch of a repackaged 146 aircraft, renamed as the RJ regional jetliner series. The RJ family comprises four variants: the RJ70, RJ85, RJ100 and RJ115. New LF507 engines provide greater thrust and can operate at cooler temperatures, increasing engine life. The RJs have all-digital avionics and a new, wider 'Spaceliner' interior, permitting larger overhead storage space and more aisle width at head height. Existing 146 orders have been transferred to the RJ orderbook.

BAe ATP

The BAe ATP is an advanced turboprop airliner, carrying 64-72 passengers on short-haul routes. It first flew in 1986 and is being used by operators in Europe, America and Asia. The ATP offers advanced technology in the 64- to 72-seat range. New standards of engine and propeller design have resulted in an exceptionally quiet cabin interior, while the six-bladed propellers' slow rotation increases efficiency and reduces noise.

Jetstream 31 and 41

The Jetstream 31 is BAe's 18- to 19-seat commuter airliner, also available in executive and business charter (and military communications) versions. Orders and options have been placed for more than 400 Jetstream 31s and Super 31s (with upgraded engines) since the Jetstream 31's first flight in 1982. More than 150 Jetstream 31s are currently in service in North America. The Jetstream Super 31 is powered by engines with increased thermodynamic power. Structural changes in the wing roots provide more fuel capacity and reduce aircraft weight, permitting increased maximum take-off weight.

The latest addition to the BAe family of regional turboprop pressurised airliners is the Jetstream 41, a 29-seat development of the Jetstream 31 that has won 117 commitments since it first flew in 1991.

Other Commercial Aircraft

Short Brothers has specialised in short-haul commercial aircraft since the mid-1960s. These included Skyvan, then the world's largest light aircraft, and the wide-body 330 30-seat and 360 36-seat regional airliners, hundreds of which have been bought by regional and international carriers. The 360 has been phased out of production. The 330-360 was based on the 360 and its predecessor, the 330, and provided increased cruising speed, high fuel efficiency and lower operating costs.

Shorts is a partner in manufacturing the 50-seat Canadair Regional Jet airliner, which had its maiden flight in 1991. It is the first turbofan airliner to be developed specifically for regional operation. Two versions of the aircraft, the standard series 100 and an extended range 100ER, are due to enter service later in 1992. Shorts has designed and manufactured the centre section of the fuselage, wing flaps, and other components.

Shorts is a risk-sharing partner with Fokker of Holland and Deutsche Airbus of Germany in the Fokker 100 jetliner, with responsibility for design and production of the aircraft's wings. Advanced composites are used in manufacturing the wing components in order to save weight and reduce manufacturing costs. The

Fokker 100 entered service with Swissair in 1988. The 150th wing set was shipped to Fokker in early 1992.

Boeing has been an important Shorts customer for 18 years. Shorts is currently sole supplier of high-technology components for the 737, 747 and 757 airliners and has recently secured a contract for the 777.

General Aviation

British Aerospace's BAe 125 is a world leader in the mid-size cabin class of business jets. Two versions are produced, one with intercontinental range. Both offer spacious accommodation with stand-up headroom for eight or more passengers, and have been improved aerodynamically. Sales total over 800, making it Britain's most successful commercial jet aircraft. BAe has decided to offer a majority stake in its Corporate Jets division to a partner.

Pilatus Britten-Norman manufactures versions of the versatile and highly successful Islander light aircraft, which seats up to ten people and can operate from short and rough airstrips. Over 1,100 have been delivered worldwide. The Turbine Islander gives improved performance in hot climatic conditions and at high altitudes. Chichester Miles is developing the Leopard, a four-seat business jet.

Several smaller aircraft are in production or under development. Lovaux manufactures the Optica Scout, a three-seat observation aeroplane that can fly as slowly as 90 km/h (56 mph), and the Venture primary trainer. The Optica Scout's exceptional field of view makes it ideal for pipeline and powerline inspection, forestry, aerial photography and policing.

Slingsby Aviation produces several versions of the T67 Firefly two-seat training and aerobatic aircraft for military and civilian customers. The 50-year-old company, best known for its range of gliders and powered gliders, supplies small components as well as complete aircraft, airships and hovercraft (see p. 52). The T67 Firefly is the first aerobatic training aircraft to be built from glass-reinforced plastic.

Several other British companies also develop and manufacture microlight aircraft, gliders and sailplanes, hang-gliders and hot-air balloons.

Military Aircraft

The British aerospace industry has achieved many outstanding successes in this area, such as the Hunter fighter, Jaguar strike aircraft, Canberra bomber and the Jet Provost trainer.

British Aerospace expanded its defence sector following BAC's successful involvement with Saudi Arabia in the 1960s. It is able to offer a complete, 'turnkey' air defence package. The company is heavily engaged in V/STOL and high performance combat aircraft. BAe technology was used widely in the Gulf War, when 18 Tornado squadrons and four Jaguar squadrons were deployed by the RAF.

Even where production has ended, export sales of refurbished aircraft continue. As a result of defence cutbacks during the early 1990s, British Aerospace set up a new company, British Aerospace Defence Ltd. This combines all defence activities previously carried out by its Military Aircraft division, two systems and dynamics divisions, and Royal Ordnance, the state-owned arms and munitions company taken over by BAe in 1987. On its own, BAe Defence is Britain's largest exporting company.

Fighter/Attack Aircraft

Tornado

BAe's most important military production programme is the Tornado combat aircraft, which entered RAF service in 1981. Export sales of Tornado to Saudi Arabia included the largest ever export contract awarded in the industry, valued at more than

£5,000 million. Tornados have also been sold to the air forces of Germany and Italy. This supersonic all-weather combat aircraft is built by Panavia Aircraft GmbH, a company set up jointly by British Aerospace, Alenia of Italy and Deutsche Aerospace of Germany.

The Tornado offers versatility of operation with minimal induced drag for short take-off and landing. It is equipped with the most advanced integrated avionics systems and fly-by-wire control system. Each of its two RB199 turbofan engines has a dry thrust of 9,000 lb, boosted to 16,000 lb with afterburning.

More than 900 Tornados are in service; there are three versions. The Tornado GR1 interdictor strike (IDS) version is designed to fly at transonic speeds (between Mach 0.8 and Mach 1.4) and carries a weapon load in excess of 7,258 kg (16,000 lb). The Tornado electronic combat and reconnaissance (ECR) version is based on the IDS. The F3 air defence variant (ADV) has been developed for the RAF as a long-range interceptor. It has a longer fuselage to accommodate more fuel and is equipped with four Sky Flash and four Sidewinder air-to-air missiles.

Harrier

The British Aerospace Harrier, which entered service with the RAF in 1969, is the only operational vertical/short take-off and landing fighter in the Western world. It has revolutionised the concept of air power on land and sea. Its Rolls-Royce Pegasus engine has rotating nozzles enabling thrust to be vectored: downwards for vertical take-off and landing; backwards for conventional flight; halfway for short take-off; and partially forwards for braking in flight or taxiing backwards.

Designed to operate from small unprepared fields, such as grass fields or heavily bombed runways, the Harrier can fly in almost any conditions. Its four nozzles enable the aircraft to decelerate rapidly or to increase its turn rate, giving it a unique advantage in combat. It is in service with the RAF, the United States Marine Corps and other overseas naval forces.

The improved Harrier II, which entered squadron service with the US Marine Corps in 1983, has been developed jointly with McDonnell Douglas in the United States. Featuring extensive carbon fibre composite sections and other aerodynamic improvements, the aircraft is designed to have double the radius of action or carry twice the ordnance compared with its predecessors. It is being upgraded to fly and fight at low altitudes by night as well as by day.

BAe's Sea Harrier is operated by the Royal Navy (RN) and the Indian Navy, aboard light aircraft carriers. RN Sea Harriers, designated FRS 1, provided combat air patrol and initial ground attack missions during the Falklands campaign in 1982. An upgrade programme is under way to bring the FRS 1 to FRS 2 standard. This can engage a number of targets simultaneously well beyond visible range, and can detect fast-moving targets flying at low level over a cluttered background, due to its new Ferranti Blue Vixen radar and advanced medium-range air-to-air missiles (AMRAAM).

European Fighter Aircraft
Together with Alenia, Deutsche Aerospace and Construcciones Aeronauticas SA of Spain, British Aerospace is a partner in the Eurofighter Company, Eurofighter Jagdflugzeug GmbH, which was established in Munich, Germany, to develop the high-technology European Fighter Aircraft (EFA) for use by NATO air forces from the late 1990s. Its development stems from the four nations'

original need to replace their existing air-defence fighters by the late 1990s with an agile, high-performance aircraft capable of meeting any airborne threat. It is the biggest programme of its kind ever undertaken in Europe and has stimulated research into new structures and materials, expert systems and artificial intelligence.

The EFA is designed for air-to-air combat and is capable of fulfilling offensive support ground attack missions. It incorporates computer-controlled 'unstable' aerodynamics, multitarget radar, a fly-by-wire control system and a throttle-and-stick control enabling the pilot to perform some 24 functions by fingertip control. It will be capable of speeds in level flight in excess of Mach 1.8 and will be able to sustain supersonic speed on the turn.

BAe's manufacturing responsibility is for the front fuselage and the leading edges of the starboard wing. The second of seven development aircraft being assembled at the BAe Warton plant is now nearing completion. The second prototype to be completed at Warton will be the first to have a full avionics complement, including advanced GEC Ferranti radar. BAe is building 15 front fuselages in all—seven for flying aircraft and eight test specimens.

The Experimental Aircraft Programme (EAP) is a technology demonstrator aircraft developed by British Aerospace with Aeritalia as a flying test rig for the EFA. The first new fighter to be flight-tested in Britain since the Lightning, it was extremely manoeuvrable and featured several innovations, including a new bonding process for carbon-fibre composites. Most of the conventional cockpit instruments were replaced by multifunction television displays.

Since April 1992, statements by the German Minister of Defence have indicated that he does not intend Germany to participate in the production phases of EFA starting in 1993.

Subsequently, however, Germany affirmed its intention to complete the development phase of the programme.

The partner nations have agreed to look at ways of significantly reducing the cost of the aircraft. A technical and military study of alternatives was to be completed before the end of 1992, before any final decisions are taken.

Trainer/Light Attack Aircraft

Hawk

The BAe Hawk is a tandem two-seat jet trainer and ground-attack aircraft used by the RAF since 1976 for advanced flying and weapons training. Around 750 have been ordered worldwide. The Hawk is transonic (up to Mach 1.2 in a dive) and is extremely manoeuvrable. Its combat capability has been enhanced by its being able to operate with Sidewinder and other types of air-to-air missiles. Three types of Hawk aircraft are built and assembled by BAe: the 100 series of two-seat advanced trainer/attack aircraft, the 200 Series of single-seat combat aircraft, and the 60 Series of two-seat trainer light attack aircraft.

The Hawk 100 is equipped with advanced navigation and attack avionics and an updated Rolls-Royce Adour turbofan engine. The Hawk 200 is a single-seat, all-weather variant of the original aircraft. It has a range of avionic and sensor equipment for combat air patrol, ground attack and interception, reconnaissance and maritime strike. Up to 300 T-45A Goshawk (Hawk variant) aircraft are being manufactured with McDonnell Douglas for the US Navy. India has selected the British Aerospace Hawk MK60 series to fulfil the combined Indian Air Force/Navy requirement for an initial 105 advanced jet trainers. The total value of the deal, including the undertaking of licensed manufacture, is around $18,400 million; deliveries are due to begin in 1993.

Shorts Tucano

Derived from the Brazilian Embraer EMB 312, the Shorts Tucano basic trainer is a new-generation aircraft now in service with the RAF and overseas. It has been specifically developed by Shorts as an advanced turboprop trainer to meet the exacting requirements of the RAF, combining high performance with cost-effectiveness. The aircraft has a level flight top speed of 270 knots, outstanding aerobatic capability, high fuel efficiency and a 12,000-hour fatigue life. It uses only half the fuel and a third of the maintenance man-power of the jet it replaces in the RAF training programme and provides the student pilot with a complete basic flight profile.

The export variant of the Shorts Tucano incorporates enhanced avionics, improved air conditioning and the option of carrying external stores. It provides a platform for weapon training and offers a highly effective counter-insurgency capability.

Other Military Aircraft

BAe has designed military variants of its 125 business jet, the P134 and P135. The P134, a signals intelligence aircraft, is designed to receive and analyse communications, electronic and radar transmissions, and relay information in near-real time back to a ground station. It can intercept signals from ground stations over 400 km (248 miles) away. The P135 is designed for monitoring surface targets from high altitude.

The military variant of the Advanced Turboprop (ATP) is the P132, a maritime patrol aircraft with anti-surface vessel and anti-submarine warfare capabilities. Fitted with advanced radar and imaging systems, the P132 can patrol for over five hours while 300 miles from base.

Military variants of Short Brothers' wide-body aircraft include the C-23 Sherpa freighters. This series of light transport aircraft are variants of Shorts' civil wide-body aircraft. Sherpas are in service with the US Air Force and Army National Guard. Intended to move ordnance, paratroops and wheeled vehicles, they can be used for other duties such as maritime or border patrols.

Pilatus Britten-Norman produces a military version of the Islander known as the Defender, which is used for airborne early warning, surveillance and fisheries protection. The maritime Defender can carry Sea Skua missiles or lightweight torpedoes.

Guided Weapons

British Aerospace and Short Brothers are responsible for a large proportion of guided weapons developed and manufactured in Britain, although several other companies work in this field. Besides being the major supplier to Britain's armed forces, BAe's Dynamics Division exports around 70 per cent of its output. It produces a range of naval gunfire control systems which has been extended to cover low-cost air defence gun sights.

All the missile systems described below are manufactured by British Aerospace, unless otherwise stated.

Air-launched Weapons

Sky Flash is an all-weather medium-range air-to-air missile guided by radar. Its radar homing system was the first of its kind in service in the Western world, enabling it to hit low-flying targets against the clutter of ground radar signals. It can be fired from aircraft flying at subsonic and supersonic speeds under all flight conditions. Used to arm Phantom and Tornado aircraft, Sky Flash is in service with the RAF and the Swedish Air Force. A new version of this missile, which operates autonomously after launch, is under development.

BAe has been awarded a £570 million contract by the British Government to design and build ASRAAM (advanced short-range air-to-air missile) for equipping Harrier jump jets and, later, the European Fighter Aircraft. The missile will be capable of operating effectively with the high acceleration encountered in air combat and will offer a significant increase in firepower.

The Sea Skua is a lightweight all-weather anti-ship missile that skims the surface of the sea to avoid detection by radar. It can be launched from helicopters such as the Westland Lynx, or from fixed-wing aircraft, and is in service with three overseas naval forces.

The Sea Eagle is an air-launched sea-skimming anti-ship missile. Guided by radar which discriminates between multiple systems, it can make long-range attacks on large warships equipped with advanced air defences and electronic counter-measure systems. It is fitted to the Royal Navy's Sea Harriers and the Indian Navy's Sea Kings. BAe's air-launched anti-radar missile, ALARM, is in service on Tornado GR1 aircraft and is being supplied to the Royal Saudi Air Force.

Surface-launched Weapons

The Rapier surface-to-air missile provides a highly mobile defence against all types of low-flying aircraft, from helicopters to land-skimming supersonic ground-attack aircraft. Its surveillance radar can detect targets from ground level to heights exceeding 900 km (3,000 ft), and at distances exceeding 11.5 km (7 miles). In service with the RAF for more than 12 years, it is one of the most successful British weapon systems, more than 21,000 having been built.

A new variant with greater firepower, Rapier Darkfire, uses an infra-red tracker which enables it to operate at night as well as in daylight. Rapier Laserfire incorporates an automatic laser tracker and is mounted on a palletised turntable. The Tracked Rapier is the first missile-armed vehicle capable of pre-empting attacks from hostile anti-tank helicopters and strike aircraft. The Rapier 2000 is an advanced version currently being developed, which will serve as the RAF's main low-level area air defence system well into the next century. Providing all-weather air defence against attack from ground-hugging supersonic ground attack aircraft, helicopters, or cruise missiles, it has a Siemens Plessey surveillance radar capable of tracking as many aircraft as Heathrow Airport. It is the first such system that can handle two targets at once. A new variant, Laserfire, which uses the same Rapier missile, has been developed by BAe.

The Seawolf, two versions of which are in service with Royal Navy frigates, is a fully automatic all-weather close area defence weapon for naval vessels. Propelled by a solid fuel rocket motor which accelerates the missile to supersonic speed, it can intercept small supersonic rockets and objects as small as 4.5-inch shells fired from naval guns. A lightweight version of Seawolf is fitted to the Royal Navy's Invincible class carriers and Type 42 destroyers. A vertical-launch version has been developed for service on the Royal Navy's Type 23 frigates.

Sea Dart is a ship-launched medium-range missile with a range exceeding 30 km (18.6 miles) for use in all weathers against aircraft and ships. In mass production, it is used on Royal Navy destroyers and aircraft carriers.

Swingfire is a wire-guided, ground-launched anti-tank missile with a range of up to 4,000 m (13,120 ft). The first of its kind to enter operational service in the West, it is in service with the British, Belgian and Egyptian armies. Swingfire can be fired from armoured or non-armoured vehicles and from hidden launch sites. More than 39,000 have been made.

The Shorts Seacat, introduced in the early 1960s and upgraded regularly since, is still the most widely used ship-to-air missile in the world. Designed to defend ships against low-level attack by supersonic aircraft, it can destroy surface-skimming ship-to-ship missiles. A height control provides a 'cushion' between missile and sea, so that the clearance distance is controlled in all sea conditions.

Shorts currently produces the Javelin and Starburst man-portable close air defence missile systems. Designed to engage the widest range of low-level attacking aircraft or helicopters, Javelin is a variant of the earlier combat-proven Blowpipe. Because it is not a heat-seeking missile, it is effective against head-on attacking aircraft and can engage them before they can release their weapons. It first entered service with the Royal Marines and British Army in 1985 and has been adopted by several overseas forces. Starburst maintains the effective design of Javelin, but has dramatically enhanced laser guidance which substantially increases hit probability. It is immune to all known countermeasures and was in service during the Gulf War.

The Shorts Starstreak is a high-velocity close air defence system being developed for the MoD. Incorporating advances in microelectronics and metallurgy, Starstreak is capable of destroying any type of helicopter or fixed-wing ground attack aircraft and is resistant to all known countermeasures. Several Starstreak variants are being developed. Together with Boeing Aerospace, Shorts is marketing Starstreak to the US Armed Forces as a complementary system to Stinger on Boeing's Avenger.

Weapon Systems Equipment

British companies such as Marconi and Ferranti produce missile control and navigation systems, radar and countermeasure equipment, and aerial target systems. Marconi Radar Systems manufactures fire-control radars for Seawolf. Ferranti pioneered the gyroscopic gunsight; its 1515 sight is installed in more than 25 types of aircraft. The company also makes laser systems for the Tornado and the RAF's Harriers and Jaguars, providing complete data on a target's range and direction.

British Aerospace Defence, BAJ and IMI Summerfield make rocket motor hardware. Hunting Engineering provides a range of specialised air weapons, including the MLRS (multiple launch rocket system) for NATO. THORN EMI Electronics develops and manufactures bomb and missile fuses. Dowty designs and manufactures hydraulic power packs used in the missile and ammunition handling systems of the Seacat and Seawolf missiles. The company specialises in electro-hydraulic power packs for radar trackers and missile launchers such as Rapier. Frazer–Nash Defence Systems supplies aircraft weapon carriage and release systems for the Tornado.

Kidde-Graviner produces guided weapons and missile safe/arm systems whose function is to ensure a missile is safe prior to launch, and to enable the warhead to be armed at a safe distance from the launcher.

Helicopters

Britain has extensive experience in the designing and manufacturing of helicopters. Between 1945 and 1965 more than 1,500 helicopters of over 20 different designs were built. The Whirlwind and its successor, the Wessex, which Westland built under licence from Sikorsky of the United States, were the most successful. During this period around five out of every six British helicopters were built by Westland. By 1960 disparate helicopter interests had been merged into the Westland company.

Westland Helicopters, now a main subsidiary of Westland Group, is one of three Western European manufacturers and has been involved in several international partnerships to produce civil and military helicopters. The company's strengths lie in its military and civil product range and systems integration capability, which enables military helicopters to be configured and equipped to meet precise operational roles.

Collaboration among helicopter companies continues to be a vital factor in future development. Westland has maintained a 45-year relationship with Sikorsky, and in 1967 began a collaborative programme with Aérospatiale of France to develop and manufacture advanced helicopters, while Rolls-Royce joined Turboméca to produce the engines. Three models have been built: the Lynx, Puma and Gazelle. More than 2,500 helicopters have been manufactured under the programme. The most important current project is the EH101 programme.

Lynx

Westland has design leadership in the Lynx, over 380 of which have been sold to ten countries. The Lynx is a general-purpose naval and military helicopter. The Super Lynx, a multi-role small ship helicopter, has advanced avionics systems and 360-degree radar. The only helicopter designed specifically for operation from small ships in rough weather, Super Lynx is equipped for autonomous operation against submarines and surface vessels, and for search and rescue. The latest Lynx development, Battlefield Lynx, is an all-weather battlefield support helicopter with advanced composite main rotors developed by Westland.

Lynx rotors incorporate British Experimental Rotor Programme (BERP) blades, which improve efficiency by up to 40 per cent. Composite blades also increase agility and reduce maintenance. Using these blades, a modified Lynx set a new world speed record for helicopters of 400 km/h (249 mph) in 1986. For overseas customers Westland is also retrofitting helicopters with composite blades.

Sea King and Black Hawk

The Westland Sea King helicopter is built under licence from Sikorsky. Over 300 Sea Kings and Commandos (the utility variant) have been sold worldwide. Intended for anti-submarine and search-and-rescue roles as well as troop and cargo transport and casualty evacuation, the Sea King can also be equipped with air-to-surface missiles for anti-surface vessel operations. Westland also has a licence to build and sell the Sikorsky S-70A Black Hawk twin-turbine utility and combat/assault helicopter. Black Hawk has proved effective in its roles as tactical transport helicopter, weapon carrier, search-and-rescue and medical evacuation. The Westland-developed version has the firepower of a modern fighter, as well as improved range and communications.

EH101

The advanced technology EH101 helicopter, which made its maiden flight in 1987, is being built in partnership with Agusta of Italy. Nine aircraft are currently flying as part of an extensive development programme.

The EH101 has a five-bladed main rotor with BERP blades of composite materials and advanced aerofoil section. The civil version, offering a high level of safety from a three-engine configuration, is designed primarily for offshore oil support operations and will carry 30 passengers over a range of 925 km (580 miles).

The military utility version has a rear loading ramp for vehicles and cargo, or can carry up to 30 troops within a 300-km (186-mile) radius of action. It can also be configured for search and rescue operations. The naval version is designed for long-range maritime patrols, anti-submarine warfare (ASW), surveillance, amphibious operations or search and rescue operations. The Royal Navy has ordered 44 Merlin anti-submarine EH101s from IBM, which has won the prime contractor role for this order. The Italian Navy has also ordered the ASW EH101 and the Canadian Government has announced its intention to order a total of 50 helicopters, to be delivered in the mid to late 1990s. A world market of 800 EH101s is anticipated.

Hovercraft and Airships

Hovercraft

Britain pioneered the development of hovercraft and is a world leader in their technology and production. Modern hovercraft are capable of speeds of up to 128 km/h (80 mph) over land, water and marshy surfaces. Well established as passenger ferries, they are also suited for coastal rescue services and a range of military roles, being relatively invulnerable to underwater defences and mines, and attack by torpedoes.

The pioneering company, Saunders-Roe, began hovercraft work in 1958. After becoming the British Hovercraft Corporation (BHC), it became part of Westland in 1959. The first civil hovercraft to go into passenger service was the SRN2 in 1962. Between 1964 and 1982 a range of SRN5 and SRN6 craft were constructed for civil and military purposes. BHC is now a subsidiary of Westland Aerospace, building hovercraft which range from large commercial craft to those with seating for fewer than ten passengers. The company also develops hovercraft components, such as skirt systems and lift fans.

In the 1970s BHC's SRN4 craft carried around a quarter of all car and passenger traffic on the cross-Channel route from the port of Dover. The company's SRN4 Mk 3 is the world's largest hovercraft. Operating on cross-Channel services, it can carry over 400 passengers and 50 cars. The diesel-powered AP1-88, in passenger service in Scandinavian countries, is designed to operate in severe winter conditions. The 55-passenger SRN6, first operated as a passenger ferry in Scandinavia in 1966, is used in the oil industry for seismic survey work. A mine countermeasure military version of the AP1-88 is being developed. The military BH-7 was first built for the Royal Navy in 1969 and is virtually immune to underwater explosions.

Amphibious hovercraft manufactured by Slingsby Aviation are suited to several roles, including passenger transport, cargo, all-weather transport, ambulance and rescue, and surveying. Formed in the 1930s, Slingsby Aviation moved from the design and manufacture of gliders to hovercraft and airship production. As well as designing and building craft, the company assesses weather conditions likely to be encountered and determines the viability of routes.

Slingsby currently builds the SAH 2200, a fully amphibious hovercraft capable of speeds of up to 40 knots and designed for civil and military purposes. Its composite construction ensures reliable operation over difficult surfaces such as mud, reefs, ice and snow. It is used as an ice breaker to keep harbours open and to free boats trapped by ice, as well as for cargo movement on to previously unreachable islands.

Hovermarine International produces 'surface effect ships' for use as ferries, coastguard patrol vessels and fireboats, while Griffon Hovercraft's production includes the 2000TDX, a 10-seat single diesel-engined craft.

Airships

Most modern airships are helium-filled, semi- or non-rigid craft with gas envelopes made from advanced polyester fabrics, and are fitted with fly-by-wire primary flight controls. They are used for aerial advertising and for filming major events, as well as for general surveillance duties, coastguard, search and rescue, detection of oil pollution, airborne early warning, and electronic and mine countermeasures.

Britain's airship industry continues to play a leading role in world airship development and manufacture. There are five principal airship companies.

The Advanced Airship Corporation is currently building an advanced non-rigid (ANR) airship, designed to fulfil both civil (essentially tourism and civil flights) and defence (primarily as surveillance and sensor platform) roles. The ANR is a quiet airship with a cruising speed of 144 km/h (90 mph), with spacious accommodation for up to 28 passengers, or equipment.

Originally the main sub-contractor to Airship Industries, Slingsby Aviation acquired the rights to the successful and technically advanced Skyship range following the collapse of the company in 1990. These airships are chiefly for civil use but have considerable potential for maritime surveillance and as early warning platforms. They are designed to make extensive use of high-strength, lightweight materials, glass-reinforced plastics and advanced composites. The engines drive vectored-thrust ducted propellers which can be swivelled through a 200-degree arc, giving the airship V/STOL and hovering capability.

In 1986 the Skyship 500 became the first airship to operate a scheduled passenger service for nearly 50 years. It can carry seven passengers at a cruising speed of 87 km/h (54 mph) over a range of 870 km (541 miles). The Skyship 600 is a 'stretched' version of the 500 with improved performance.

Thunder and Colt makes the ANR envelope as well as a range of hot-air and helium airships, including the largest hot-air airship ever flown. It also manufactures hot-air balloons. Cameron

The Shorts Sunderland entered service with the RAF in 1938. One of the most successful military flying-boats ever built, it continued in service for over 20 years.

Equipping Airbus A321 wingboxes at the British Aerospace (BAe) site at Filton. The first A321 flight is scheduled for early 1993.

The four-engined Airbus A340, the world's longest-range civil airliner.

Complete wings for the Fokker 100 jetliner under construction at Shorts in Belfast.

The BAe 146–300. One of the world's quietest airliners, it is ideally suited to operate in and out of noise-sensitive airports.

A Shorts-built nose cowl fitted to an RB211 engine at Rolls-Royce's Derby plant.

A Rolls-Royce Trent 800 turbofan, one of the world's most advanced aero-engines, under inspection. With the highest thrust (up to 100,000 lb) of the series, over 40 per cent of production is destined for the Airbus A330. The Trent has also captured 28 per cent of the Boeing 777 market and is offered on the McDonnell Douglas MD-12.

The BAe Sea Harrier FRS 2 in service with the Royal Navy, shown flying with four advanced medium-range air-to-air missiles.

The Pegasus 11 vectored-thrust turbofan, built by Rolls-Royce to power the Harrier and AV-8 series of verticle/short take-off and landing aircraft.

GEC Avionics' 'Knighthelm' helmet-mounted display. Designed for day and night operations, it projects both light-intensified images and forward-looking infra-red (FLIR) imagery onto clear glass eye-pieces in front of the pilot's eyes.

The Shorts Tucano high-performance turboprop trainer under construction. It has a strengthened wing structure, to increase the airframe's fatigue life to 12,000 flights, and a cockpit compatible with that of the RAF's advanced Hawk trainer to ease the transition from basic to advanced training.

Mark 10A ejection seat supplied by Martin-Baker for the Panavia Tornado. Capable of providing safe escape at altitudes above 50,000 feet, the Mark 10A saved 10 aircrew lives during the Gulf War.

Constructed from highly advanced composite materials, these swept-tip rotor blades designed for the Westland Lynx helicopter have a greatly increased lift capacity and a longer fatigue life than those manufactured in conventional metals.

GEC Sensors' ATLANTIC pod, employing the company's modular FLIR system, provides attack aircraft with night and poor weather visibility for high-speed, low-level missions.

The T67M 200 Firefly military trainer, manufactured by Slingsby Aviation for the Royal Hong Kong Auxiliary Air Force.

Didsbury Engineering manufactures equipment for various ground support roles, including main engine changes.

Artist's impression of the European Space Agency (ESA) Ulysses mission to the poles of the Sun. The probe's British-made instruments have been used to investigate the magnetic field of Jupiter.

TDS 4 is a fully transportable, self-contained satellite earth-station built by BAe for the ESA to transmit experimental and educational material to its Olympus satellite, which re-broadcasts them, at a different frequency, to a pre-determined area of Europe.

Miniature mechanical cryogenic coolers
under test at BAe (Space Systems), Bristol.
These lightweight units are used to cool the
detector elements of sensitive instruments
on board scientific and earth observation
spacecraft, such as the Polar Orbiting
Platform due for launch in the late 1990s.

Navigation antenna being tested for the
planned Inmarsat-3 series at Matra Marconi
Space (UK), Portsmouth.

Balloons is principally a hot-air balloon manufacturer, and is also the first company to develop hot-air airships. It currently produces small 1- to 2-seater hot-air and helium airships. Ferranti International is also making a range of airships for airborne surveillance.

Space Activities

Over 200 British companies take part in national and international space programmes. They range from major companies employing many thousands to medium-sized and small specialist technology companies. Most international programmes are undertaken by consortia of companies from the 13 member states of the European Space Agency (ESA). In 1964 the SBAC changed its name from Society of British Aircraft Constructors to Society of British Aerospace Companies, reflecting the industry's expansion into the manufacture of vehicles and systems for space applications. Since then, British aerospace companies have been engaged in producing a range of satellites, in the design and construction of 100 associated earth stations all round the world, and in manufacturing sounding rockets, used to carry scientific and Earth observation payloads into space for very short periods.

The Government is a major customer of space systems. It promotes the growth of the space industry by funding key technologies and space missions, and developing facilities for the industry to use in their development and operation. Government finance supports research in space sciences undertaken by universities and other higher education institutions.

The range of services offered by the industry includes system specification and design, subsystem and space segment development, initial consultancy and market analysis, and the provision of total systems packages for civil and military communications, remote sensing, meteorology and scientific satellites. British companies supply ground facilities required by meteorological and remote sensing satellites, and are developing technologies to ensure that electronic equipment and antenna designs operate effectively under all environmental conditions.

A major activity of companies is the production of satellite systems and payloads. They also make power supply, attitude (orientation of spacecraft) measurement and control, telemetry (coded transmission by radio or telephony) and command, data management, antennae, and a host of other subsystems. These companies have developed specialised skills and components which are used by satellite and subsystem designers. Matra Marconi Space, for example, is a joint Anglo-French company specialising in spacecraft, payloads and instrumentation and communications terminals.

British National Space Centre

Support for civil space research is co-ordinated by the British National Space Centre (BNSC), a partnership between various government departments and research councils. This body encourages industry to exploit opportunities for space applications and provides links with the ESA and other international space organisations. Formed in 1985 to be a focus for Britain's civil space effort within government and to act as the main channel for government support to British companies conducting R & D, the BNSC contributes to the ESA's many scientific, telecommunications, and Earth observation programmes. Through the BNSC, Britain spent some £158 million on space activities in 1991–92, of which over 60 per cent was devoted to ESA programmes.

Scientific Research

In space science, Britain has taken part in almost all ESA missions, including the encounter with Halley's Comet in 1986; the

International Ultraviolet Explorer; the Hipparcos star-mapping mission; and the Ulysses solar polar probe, which used British-made instruments to investigate the magnetic field of Jupiter.

Two important scientific programmes currently involving Britain are the Cluster and Solar Heliospheric Observatory (SOHO) missions due to be launched in 1995 to study the Sun, the Earth's magnetosphere and the solar wind. British experiments have provided information that has increased scientific knowledge significantly, especially in astronomy and astrophysics, and in interpreting climatic patterns.

Britain has bilateral arrangements for space research with other countries, such as the United States through NASA, the Commonwealth of Independent States, and the People's Republic of China. It has participated in several NASA space science missions and British companies have developed instruments for NASA's Hubble Space Telescope. In 1991 Britain's first astronaut, Helen Sharman, took part in a mission of the Soviet Mir space station, during which she carried out a number of scientific experiments in orbit. Other collaborations include the development of the Wide-Field Camera for Germany's X-ray satellite ROSAT and the X-ray sensor for the Japanese-built Ginga satellite.

British Aerospace's experience as a prime contractor in scientific space programmes dates from 1967. It was prime contractor on the ESA's Giotto spacecraft which intercepted Halley's Comet in 1986 and Comet Grigg-Skjellerup in 1992, following an extended mission. BAe built part of the Faint Object Camera for the Hubble Space Telescope and solar panels for the ESA/NASA telescope launched in 1990. BAe also supplied equipment to the ESA Ulysses satellite mission to Jupiter and the Sun, and for the Hipparcos satellite, built for ESA under the prime contractorship of Matra

Marconi Space to map the positions of 100,000 stars. Both companies are involved in preparing SOHO.

Communications Satellites

European Communications Satellites

Britain has capitalised on commercial opportunities generated by the ESA satellite communications programmes. British Aerospace has been the prime contractor for ESA's communications satellite programmes since 1978, manufacturing four satellites for the agency's European Communications Satellite (ECS) series, Europe's indigenous satellite telecommunications network. Each satellite can handle 12,600 telephone circuits and two television transmissions, as well as telex and facsimile transmissions. BAe was also prime contractor for Olympus, ESA's multi-role satellite launched in 1989 and the largest 3-axis stabilised civil communications satellite built in Europe. Its specialised services payload was developed by Matra Marconi Space.

The European satellite communications network, including the ECS satellites, is operated by the Eutelsat consortium, representing 27 countries. Matra Marconi Space is the communications payload contractor for the Eutelsat 2 series of satellites.

Intelsat and Inmarsat

Britain is a founder member of the International Telecommunications Satellite Organisation, Intelsat, which transmits telephone and television services between ground stations worldwide. British Aerospace supplied equipment for the Intelsat III, IV and V series of satellites, and was a major subcontractor in an international team for the five Intelsat VI satellites.

Britain is the second largest shareholder in the International Maritime Satellite Organisation, Inmarsat, which co-ordinates global maritime communications. BAe was the prime contractor for Marecs A and B2 satellites, which have been operating over the Atlantic and Pacific oceans, and for which Matra Marconi Space supplied the communications payload.

BAe was also prime contractor for Inmarsat 2, which has four times the capacity of Marecs; all four satellites have been launched and are operational. Matra Marconi Space will supply the communications payload for the planned Inmarsat 3 series. It features a navigation package designed as a civil complement to the US navigational Global Position System.

Remote Sensing

Remote sensing satellites collect physical data about the Earth's surface and upper atmosphere. The development of remote sensing products and services derived from that data is the centrepiece of current government support for the application of space technology.

Remote sensing products are of potential use to organisations involved in oil and mineral exploration, civil engineering, agriculture, forestry, the environment, urban planning, coastal monitoring and oceanography. Available in both digital and photographic formats, products include raw data, satellite image maps, and specially enhanced material where geometric distortion has been corrected.

A typical Earth observation system consists of a 'space segment' (platform and payload) and a 'ground segment' (control station, data reception and transmission, ground processing, and archiving centre and distribution centre). British Aerospace and

Matra Marconi Space have total systems capability, from satellites and ground stations to the provision of image processing facilities. The BNSC plays a major part in ESA Earth observation programmes. Areas of particular expertise are the design and manufacture of satellite systems, instrumentation and data processing.

ESA Programmes

Britain has a substantial role in the ESA's European Remote Sensing satellite (ERS-1) programme. ERS-1, launched in 1991, is the first European satellite to carry a 'suite' of microwave instruments providing all-weather day and night observation of the Earth's surface. Britain has committed around £75 million to the project.

ERS-1's Active Microwave Instrument (AMI) was designed and built by Matra Marconi Space. This includes a Synthetic Aperture Radar, which produces images by integrating data from successive antenna positions, making use of a larger effective aperture—a 'synthetic aperture'—to provide very high resolution. Matra Marconi Space also manufactured the attitude and orbit control systems, onboard software, and electrical ground support equipment associated with the spacecraft. Its Along Track Scanning Radiometer (ATSR) for measuring sea surface temperature was built by a consortium led by the Rutherford Appleton Laboratory.

Britain will continue to have an important role in future remote sensing programmes. Matra Marconi Space is providing an AMI for ERS-2. British Aerospace, together with the Rutherford Appleton Laboratory, will supply a more advanced version of the ATSR flown on ERS-1. BAe is also prime contractor for the design and manufacture of the ESA Polar Platform. This polar-orbiting Earth observation satellite is Europe's contribution to Columbus, the US-led international space station project, Freedom, due for completion around the end of the century.

National Remote Sensing Centre
The National Remote Sensing Centre (NRSC) was set up at Farnborough in 1980 to promote the benefits, applications and techniques of satellite remote sensing in Britain. It is funded by the DTI and is one of Europe's leading suppliers of Earth observation imagery, products and services. Its primary role is to introduce new users in industry, government departments and academic institutions to satellite imagery and to demonstrate how the data can be used for a variety of applications. The Centre sells computer-processed images from Landsat, the US satellite series, ERS-1, and the French commercial satellite, SPOT. It also offers scientific consultancy and systems engineering services.

Earth Observation Data Centre
The Earth Observation Data Centre (EODC), inaugurated in 1991, is a specialist data centre equipped to process, archive and disseminate data from the ESA's ERS-1 and other satellites. The EODC complex incorporates the United Kingdom Processing and Archiving Facility—one of four such European facilities for handling data from ERS-1.

The National Remote Sensing Centre has been absorbed by NRSC Ltd and is working, through BNSC and the Defence Research Agency, to make EODC facilities available for commercial use. Typical products are data tapes, computer-processed pictures of Earth, map products, information services, consultancy and systems engineering services.

The Government has invested some £30 million in the complex during the last ten years, and has provided NRSC Ltd with a

£9.6 million commercialisation contract to help the company achieve full independent commercial operation by 1996. Industry will continue to invest resources to ensure the long-term success of the venture.

Space Transportation and Systems

British Aerospace carries out overall systems design for launch vehicles, as well as producing propellant and pressurisation control systems, and launcher release equipment. It also made spacelab pallets for the US space shuttle programme. Contributions by British companies towards the ESA Ariane satellite launcher programme include the Ariane and dual launch structure, SPELDA, the Vehicle Equipment Bay for Ariane 5, and engine propellant and ducting systems.

In conjunction with the British National Space Centre and Rolls-Royce, British Aerospace has carried out studies for an advanced single-stage-to-orbit launch vehicle (HOTOL—horizontal take off and landing). A British concept, HOTOL is envisaged as a low-cost, unmanned launch vehicle carrying satellites into low Earth orbit.

Systems and Component Supply

A host of British companies design and manufacture advanced space systems and components. Matra Marconi Space is active in the full range of space technologies, from payloads to antenna subsystems and image processing. THORN EMI Electronics supplies a range of equipment for over 50 space projects. DCC produces digital satellite earth stations and terminal equipment for the Intelsat, Eutelsat and Inmarsat networks.

ERA Technology is an independent research and development organisation servicing government, industry and international agencies. It specialises in spacecraft antennas for civil and

military satellite communication networks. GEC Ferranti manufactures gyro systems and components, and inertial guidance systems for the stabilisation and control of satellites, launch vehicles
and sounding rockets.

Hunting Technical Services supplies image processing and
analysis, and consultancy services in remote sensing. Logica Space
& Defence provides onboard digital systems for satellites and
advanced software technology services. Smith Associates specialises in system analysis and communications equipment for satellites,
and advanced data processing techniques for remote sensing.

Aero-engines

Aero-engines are a vitally important sector of Britain's aerospace industry in terms of sales, export earnings and technological achievement. Rolls-Royce is renowned for its 85-year experience in the field, having pioneered the development of gas turbines for high-speed aircraft with its turbojets for the Meteor jet fighter during the second world war.

One of Britain's biggest exporters, with around three-quarters of its sales in overseas markets, its customers include over 300 airlines, 700 executive and corporate users, and more than 100 armed forces. It is one of only three companies in international markets with the capability to design, develop and manufacture gas turbine aero-engines for civil and military applications. In 1991 Rolls-Royce had nearly a quarter of the market share of civil engine orders worldwide.

International Partnerships

As in other areas of aerospace, international partnerships are increasingly important in the aero-engine business. The Adour turbofan programme for the Anglo-French Jaguar aircraft was jointly undertaken in the 1960s by Rolls-Royce and Turboméca of France.

Today, Rolls-Royce has over 160 licence and collaboration agreements and more than 20 major overseas partners. It has a 30 per cent holding in the five-nation International Aero Engines (IAE) consortium of companies. IAE is responsible for producing the V2500 low-pollution turbofan, which powers some versions of the Airbus A320 and A321 and McDonnell Douglas MD-90. Orders and options for the V2500 total more than 1,500. With Williams International, Rolls-Royce is developing the FJ44 turbofan for business and other small jets. European and Japanese partners are involved in the manufacture of the Trent engine, ordered for new wide-body airliners such as the Airbus 330 and Boeing 777.

Civil Jet Engines

RB211 series

Rolls-Royce's RB211 generation of engines are used in some 30 aircraft types (see Table 3). Engine thrusts range from 37,400 lb to 100,000 lb. The RB211 turbofan has completed nearly 45 million hours' service with airlines worldwide. More than 2,800 RB211 engines have been ordered, of which over 2,000 have been delivered.

Table 3: Gas Turbines

Type of Engine	Name	Aircraft
Turbojet	Olympus 593	Concorde
	Viper	Military aircraft
Turbofan	RB211	Boeing 747
	RB211-535	Boeing 757
	Tay	Gulfstream IV, Fokker l00
	Adour	Jaguar, Hawk
	RBl99	Tornado
Turboprop	Dart	BAe 748, Fokker F27
	Tyne	Transall C-160, Atlantic
Turboshaft	Gem	Lynx
	Gnome	Sea King

The RB211-524G and -524H, the most recent to enter service on the Boeing 747-400 and 767-300, give improved thrust and fuel efficiency and feature Rolls-Royce's unique wide-chord fan blades, together with an electronic fuel control system. A 524-G-powered Boeing 747-400 of the Australian airline, Qantas, holds the world long-distance record for a commercial aircraft, having flown from London to Sydney non-stop in 20 hours 9 minutes. The RB211-524 can be upgraded to incorporate new technological advances.

The -535C, for short- to medium-haul airliners, entered service in 1983 on the twin-engined Boeing 757 airliner. Over three-quarters of all Boeing 757 operators have chosen the -535 for their airliners. The -535E4, which entered service in 1984, has wide-chord fan blades and an advanced exhaust system. Designed for easy maintenance, it has demonstrated a 10 per cent improvement in fuel efficiency and outstanding reliability. Its exceptional quietness allows greater freedom of access to noise-sensitive airports.

The development of larger-capacity aircraft means there is a need for engines of 50,000 lb thrust or more. Already leading the market is the latest RB211 development—the Trent. The world's most powerful turbofan, rated at 65,000–85,000 lb, it is due to come into service in 1995. The Trent, too, offers improved fuel efficiency and lower maintenance costs. There are more than 200 orders and options for the Trent, to power the Airbus A330 and Boeing 777.

The Tay turbofan, which entered service in 1987, powers the Fokker 100 airliner and Gulfstream IV executive jet, and is used to re-engine other types. The Fokker 100 is economical, reliable and straightforward to maintain. More than 1,800 have been ordered.

Aero-engine Technologies
Design requirements of advanced gas turbines include increased power, minimum size and weight, improved fuel economies, and

low operating and maintenance costs. Civil aircraft engines must also maintain low levels of noise and emissions, incorporating lightweight engine components for high performance and longer life. Rolls-Royce engines hold the world record for continuous service without removal, with lead engines exceeding 22,000 hours in flight. The all-time record was over 24,000 hours, achieved by an RB211 in a Lockheed L1011 Tristar.

Using an evolutionary approach, Rolls-Royce develops engines by incorporating technical advances proven on other engines or in advanced engineering programmes. Before full-scale development begins, extensive testing is carried out using demonstrator engines. This ensures a minimum of technical and financial risk, and has allowed the progressive development of a range of engines over many years, giving extensive performance and economic benefits for customers.

The RB211 engine family exemplifies the company's derivative approach to development. The take-off thrust of RB211 engines increased by nearly a half between the early 1970s and the end of the 1980s. The RB211-535C engine was based on the proven core of the initial version of the RB211. The 535C was used to drive a smaller fan, producing greater reliability. Refinements made to the core engine for the Trent, derived from the latest RB211-524, will be available retrospectively to improve the performance of the RB211 engines powering Boeing 747 and 767 airliners.

The RB211-535E4 version introduced the unique Rolls-Royce wide-chord fan. This design features a smaller number of wider and stronger blades than fans on competing engines, giving the necessary stiffness to improve aerodynamic efficiency. It has enabled Rolls-Royce engines to produce a greater thrust from a given fan diameter, improved fuel efficiency and resistance to damage by foreign objects. Wide–chord fans have seven years of proven service and are installed on the Tay, RB211–524 and the V2500 (and the Trent when completed).

Fuel consumption has been improved through the application of computational fluid dynamics. This enables complex gas flows around components to be visualised and their design to be fine-tuned. Advanced computer-aided design, measurement and simulation techniques are used to test engine components.

Environmental Measures

Aero-engine manufacturers are working on improvements to engine design to reduce environmentally harmful emissions and noise. At present, aircraft generate around 2 per cent of global nitrogen oxide (NOx) emissions. However, some experts have predicted that the projected doubling of air traffic in the next 20 years will adversely affect the Earth's ozone layer. Rolls-Royce is modifying existing engines for short-term reductions in NOx by improving the way fuel and air is mixed prior to combustion. The company is introducing a new combustor on its future turbofan engines that sprays fuel from 24 instead of 18 nozzles to give more even fuel/air mixing and reduced combustion temperatures. It has reported that a 30 per cent reduction in NOx emission has already been demonstrated. Rolls-Royce and SNECMA of France have begun work on a new combustor intended for use on supersonic aircraft. A technology spin-off from this programme for subsonic aircraft is also envisaged.

Airport noise tends to come from older jet airliners with low-bypass turbofan engines. As all aircraft are expected to comply with new international regulations by 2002, suitable older aircraft with substantial structure life remaining are being fitted with modern, higher-bypass engines, such as the Rolls-Royce Tay. The high by-pass ratio of this engine, with its mixed exhaust system, offers reduced noise levels compared with the engines originally fitted. The RB211-524 engines powering Boeing 747s and 767s are significantly quieter than their predecessors.

Military Jet Engines

The RB199, which powers the Tornado, is produced by Turbo-Union, a joint company set up by Rolls-Royce, MTU Munich of Germany and FiatAvio of Italy. It provides very high thrust for combat manoeuvres and supersonic acceleration, coupled with low fuel consumption for long-range flying at low levels. The Pegasus turbofan engine for the V/STOL Harrier introduced the vectored-thrust principle to military aviation, its thrust more than doubling since it first entered service. The Pegasus 11 is a unique vectored-thrust turbofan powering the Harrier and AV-8 series of V/STOL aircraft. The latest version, the Pegasus 11-61, is capable of a 15 per cent increase in vertical lift thrust and has longer engine life.

The Adour twin-shaft turbofan was originally built by Rolls-Royce to power the Jaguar; the latest versions power the Hawk and T-45A Goshawk trainers. Over 5,400 Rolls-Royce Spey turbofans have been manufactured for civil and military aircraft, such as the RAF Nimrod and Phantom, and Fokker F28. The latest Spey military variant powers the AMX attack aircraft in service with the air forces of Italy and Brazil.

Military engines impose more exacting demands for sheer performance than civil engines. The EJ200 turbofan engine for the European Fighter Aircraft is designed to provide a thrust ten times its weight (around 20,000 lb). Rolls-Royce has a 33 per cent holding in the Eurojet consortium which is developing the EJ200. The company contributed technologies to the programme that were tested on its XG-40 demonstrator engine. These included single-crystal turbine blades, lightweight high-strength discs, and full-authority digital electronic control (FADEC).

Helicopter Engines

Rolls-Royce has extensive interests in this field, with three engines in production. The latest, tropicalised version of the Gnome turboshaft, which first entered service in 1961, powers the Westland Sea King and Commando. The Gem turboshaft has been in production since 1976.

The advanced RTM322 turboshaft is the result of a partnership involving Rolls-Royce, Turboméca and Piaggio. Designed to power helicopters in the 7-15 tonne class, it has been chosen to power the Royal Navy's EH101 Merlin. Rolls-Royce has also joined Turboméca and MTU Munich in the MTR390 engine programme for the Franco-German Tiger anti-tank helicopter.

Engine Components

Nacelle Systems

Shorts has specialised in the design and manufacture of engine nacelle systems and components for turbofan engines for over a quarter of a century. It pioneered the use of lightweight advanced composite materials in nacelle production and contributes to many Rolls-Royce power plant programmes.

Shorts designed and manufactured the nose cowl, fan cowl doors and engine build units for the RB211-524 engine. Over 640 engine nacelle kits have been delivered for incorporation in Boeing aircraft. The company has supplied over 380 nose cowls for the

RB211-535 variant destined for the Boeing 757. The RB211 Trent (700 series) nacelle will incorporate Shorts' lightweight nose cowls.

Complete nacelles for the four Textron Lycoming engines used on the British Aerospace BAe 146 and its successors are built by Shorts. Significant noise reduction achieved on the BAe l46 is partly due to Shorts' honeycomb-bonded aluminium nacelle panels. Over 200 aircraft sets (848 nacelle kits) have been delivered.

In collaboration with Rohr Industries of the United States, Shorts is also responsible for the design and manufacture of the nacelle for International Aero Engine's V2500 in service on the A320 Airbus. This nacelle incorporates advanced carbon fibre material and woven stainless steel wire to form a double layer of acoustic lining. The company will also supply complete nacelles for the Canadair Regional Jet and Challenger business aircraft.

Westland Aerospace, based on the Isle of Wight, specialises in the design, manufacture and qualification of engine nacelles for turboprop aircraft. It has secured over half of the anticipated production over the next five years for turboprop engine nacelles, and is to build advanced composite and metallic nacelles for the BAe Jetstream 41, Dornier 328, and the Saab 2000. For the latter programme, Westland will also integrate the nacelle's propulsion system. The company has also delivered over 700 nacelles for the de Havilland Dash 8 turboprop regional airliner.

Westland makes flight-critical flying control surfaces and turbofan nacelle structures and components for major aircraft manufacturers—Airbus Industrie, Boeing and McDonnell Douglas.

Engine Systems
Lucas Aerospace is the leading British manufacturer of fuel pumps and controls for civil and military turbines, having supplied fuel

pumping and metering equipment for the first gas turbine engines developed by Sir Frank Whittle and Rolls-Royce. Its products include high-pressure pumps, digital engine controls and thrust reversers.

Advanced fuel pump systems are in use on the RB211 engine series, providing inputs required for accurately scheduling fuel flow. Lucas developed the first electronically controlled fuel systems installed on Concorde and supplied the first Digital Engine Control Unit for the Tornado. It is devising electronic engine control systems for the new generation of turboprop, turbofan and turboshaft engines.

Lucas also designs and manufactures combustion chambers, fuel sprayers and engine management systems, and is a major supplier of ignition systems and thrust reversers. The company's Combustion Technology and Engineering Centre operates an independent consultancy in gas turbine combustion and related technology based on 40 years' experience in this field of engineering.

High-speed turbo machinery for aircraft have been developed by Normalair-Garrett since the 1950s. The company produces power plants specifically for use in unmanned, recoverable or non-recoverable aircraft. It also makes a variety of heat transfer products, such as oil coolers and surface heat exchangers.

Smiths Industries (SI) has specialised in engine control and monitoring for over 30 years and has supplied specialised units, like fibre optic high-temperature sensors for almost every type of Rolls-Royce engine.

Dowty and Smiths Industries Controls is a joint venture company merging the engine control technology of SI with the electro-mechanical control system of Dowty. The company produces afterburner controls for military engines. These feature a unique vapour core pump which supplies fuel at high pressure over a wide range of flows without high rises in temperature. It was responsible for the world's first flight of a single-engined military aircraft under full authority digital electronic control, on a Pegasus-powered Harrier.

Both Dowty and British Aerospace manufacture propellers for aircraft engines, the most advanced of which have composite blades of carbon and glass-fibre reinforced material. BAe makes large composite structure propellers for hovercraft and for wind turbine generators as well as aircraft. Dowty has made composite unducted fan blades for experimental ultra-high bypass ratio engines.

Dunlop has 80 years' experience in the production of heat exchange equipment to many of the world's aero-engine manufacturers. Vickers Precision Components undertakes investment casting, machining, fabrication, as well as service and repair of engine-run components. It specialises in producing nozzle guide vanes and turbine engine combustion liners.

Other Systems and Equipment

Some 300 British companies are engaged in producing all types of aerospace systems and equipment, and many more in related electronics. The aerospace equipment industry now exceeds the aero-engine sector in terms of turnover and is the largest in Europe. Direct exports, combined with the value of products equipping aircraft, aero-engines, missiles and space vehicles destined for export, exceeds 70 per cent of the equipment sector's total turnover.

British firms are particularly expert in the field of avionics and the production of large-scale, complex components. It is not possible to cover the full range of systems made in Britain, but several of the more important ones are described here.

Navigation Equipment

Navigation aids include those that work in conjunction with ground- or satellite-based equipment, and self-contained systems. A number of British companies are active in both areas. Several systems are based on very high frequency Omnirange (VOR), incorporating instrument landing systems (ILS) receivers. These are essentially radio systems based on ground transmitters, giving an aircraft the directional, longitudinal and vertical guidance necessary for landing. GEC Sensors, Racal, British Aerospace and Cossor Electronics are among the companies producing such systems.

Racal Avionics' ILS transmitters are in service at RAF and civil airfields in Britain and overseas. Many civil aircraft are equipped with GEC Sensors' AD 260, which also makes available guidance information for the aircraft's automatic landing system. The company's AD620K integrated navigation system provides an immediate display of present position, with key-touch guidance to any of 1,000 waypoints. Its Forward Looking Infra Red (FLIR) equipment enhances pilot vision for navigation in fast, low-level flight at night, or in poor visibility.

Many self-contained navigation systems are based on the Doppler principle, which measures the frequency variations between transmitted and reflected radio waves to produce infor- mation on the speed and direction of moving objects. Marconi was the first company to introduce Doppler navigation systems, in 1948.

GEC Sensors' current range is in use worldwide, including its AD660 Doppler Velocity Sensor in service on Boeing 737 airliners, which consists of a compact, self-contained box weighing less than 20 lb (9 kg).

Area Navigation Systems
Area navigation systems, pioneered by British companies during the second world war, are vital for making the optimum use of airspace in congested areas, particularly around airports. They include equipment for fixing aircraft positions, such as that pro- duced by Racal, and cockpit map displays, which are manufactured by GEC Ferranti and GEC Avionics.

Racal developed a navigational fixing aid which depends on a chain of radio transmitting stations, while providing fixing cover over extended areas. Racal Avionics' Doppler velocity sensor for rotary and fixed-wing aircraft, Doppler 90, has been supplied for 100 different aircraft types.

Cockpit Map Displays

GEC Avionics' Digital Video Map is a video display map which moves and rotates as the aircraft moves, showing elevations higher than the flight path, targets, and intelligence that has been programmed before take-off. Digital Video Maps are in production for the RAF Night Attack Harrier. The company's covert navigation and terrain-following system compares stored map and elevation data with flight profile information so as to fix the aircraft's position.

GEC-Plessey Avionics supplies equipment for the satellite-based Global Positioning System (GPS). Its receivers offer very high performance, updating the navigation solution ten times a second.

GEC Ferranti produces moving monochrome and colour map displays for military aircraft such as the Harrier and Tornado. The company's advanced Combined Map and Electronic Display system overlays the map image with navigational and other map-related information. These displays are fitted in the ECR Tornado and the Indian Air Force Jaguar. Companies such as GEC Ferranti are developing high-resolution electronic map generators for handling digital map data.

Inertial Navigation Systems

Inertial navigation systems were pioneered in Britain by BAe, GEC Avionics and GEC Ferranti. Developed initially for military use, they have since been adapted for large civil aircraft. Modern systems can be fitted to older airframes, prolonging their service life. British Aerospace (Systems and Equipment) is Europe's largest manufacturer of gyro compass instruments and built the first laser gyroscope inertial navigation system in 1981. An advanced version,

LINS 300, has been selected for the EH101 helicopter and the Hawk 100 and 200 aircraft.

GEC Avionics produced Britain's first inertial platform and Europe's first digital inertial system for Jaguars for RAF service and overseas. The company supplies (non-gimballed) strap-down systems, incorporating ring laser gyros and a navigation system, for the British Army.

Smiths Industries has over 40 years' experience in making gyros, including the first strap-down inertial system in the 1960s. Its Attitude and Reference systems are in operation in US military aircraft and it has supplied over 100,000 vertical and directional gyros and 100,000 rate gyros for use in all types of aircraft world-wide.

Air Data Systems

GEC Avionics has supplied 4,500 Standard Central Air Data Computers to the US Navy and Air Force. Its miniature Standard Air Data Computer range incorporates units for high-agility combat aircraft, transport aircraft and executive transports. The company, together with its partners in the European consortium, is supplying the Air Data Transducer unit for the EFA. Its Helicopter Air Data System has been selected for the EH101.

Flight Data Displays

Flight data systems record and display the various functions of an aircraft, ranging from its static or dynamic state to flight and pilot performance. The advent of avionics in the cockpit and on the flight deck, in the form of analogue circuits and the cathode-ray tube (CRT), were key technological steps in providing the main 'interface' between pilot and aircraft.

The British avionics industry, notably companies such as Smiths Industries, adapted CRT for cockpit use in the 1940s. Its first commercial application was as weather radar on the instrument panels of aircraft in the 1950s.

Head-up Display (HUD) and Other Cockpit Display Systems

In the late 1950s, following a concept developed by the Royal Aerospace Establishment, Smiths Industries and other companies combined the optical systems of gunsights with the CRT to produce the head-up display (HUD). This has proved to be a significant milestone in avionics. Projecting symbols electronically into the pilot's view ahead, the HUD provides all the information needed to fly and navigate the aircraft. This allows the pilot to focus attention on the view outside—vital when flying at high speed close to the ground and in combat situations.

The first series of HUDs was based on analogue electronics; by the 1970s, digital avionics became the standard. This particular development had strong impact on the design of the cockpit and flight deck displays. In modern combat aircraft HUD is combined with a weapon-aiming computer system (HUDWAC).

GEC Avionics is the world's largest manufacturer of HUDs and HUDWACs. Over 10,000 have been supplied worldwide for more than 50 aircraft types. It is to supply computer-generated holographic HUDs for the EFA and the F-22. Designed to minimise obstructive hardware between the pilot and the outside world, the EFA's HUD features an advanced flat panel display combining fuel gauges with displays of communications, engine data and the HUD control. A cockpit colour television sensor continuously records the outside scene for mission debriefing.

GEC Avionics also uses refractive and holographic optics to give an enhanced, wide field-of-view display. A recently developed HUD enables passenger aircraft to make approaches in poor visibility by supporting the pilot with an information display produced by weather-penetrating sensors, which are combined with aircraft guidance and navigation information from the HUD computer. The company is the world's largest supplier of night-attack HUDs.

Several British firms make cockpit instruments and displays. Smiths Industries is one of the foremost, its instruments being used by over 450 airlines and air forces. British Aerospace, Siemens Plessey and THORN EMI are among other leading manufacturers.

Head-up displays and associated systems made by SI include CRT control and display units for primary flight display, radar altimeters, flight management display panels using CRTs, head-down displays, and display computers. The company's HUDs have been fitted to many military aircraft, including the Harrier/AV8, RAF Jaguar, Tornado, and the US Navy T-45. Smiths Industries has developed a range of diffractive optical techniques to give wide field-of-view and enhanced display clarity.

HUDs for some 1,100 F-15s in service with the US Air Force and elsewhere are being developed by SI. The company's high-colour tactical displays are fitted to McDonnell Douglas F-18 and AV8B aircraft. SI is also responsible for an integrated version of the Helmet Mounted Display (HMD).

GEC Ferranti's entry into HUDs followed a long involvement with aircraft gunsights. It developed the first raster-capable HUD, which was used to enhance low-level night-flying techniques. A GEC Ferranti HUD incorporating advanced optics to achieve high brightness and wide field-of-view was selected for the Tornado mid-life update. The company has developed a range of high-brightness colour and monochrome displays for military air-craft, including the Sea Harrier II and Hawk 100/200. Its night vision goggles provide the pilot with the scene information needed to fly safely and effectively at low level and in all weathers, day or night. GEC Ferranti has devised fully integrated helmet mounted display systems.

Flight Test Instrumentation and Monitoring Systems

GEC-Plessey, one of the world's leading manufacturers in this field, supplies airlines and air forces with systems covering flight-test instrumentation, engine health and structural monitoring. Its helicopter monitoring system fulfils the functions of a digital flight data recorder, a cockpit voice recorder, and a health and usage monitoring system. Its flight data acquisition system is used on Concorde and the Boeing 747. Over 1,000 units have been built for the US Air Force.

Smiths Industries also makes fuel gauges and electrical load management systems, the latest of which will be responsible for the control, distribution and protection of fuel and electrical supplies on the Boeing 777, destined to be the world's largest twin-engine aircraft when it enters passenger service in 1995.

GEC Avionics is collaborating with German and Spanish companies to supply engine monitoring units (EMUs) for the EJ200 engines of the European Fighter Aircraft. In providing continuous monitoring of engine incidents, performance, failure detection and location, the EMU will allay the need for frequent maintenance checks.

The company is a leading supplier of airborne computing systems for civil and military aircraft. It developed the mission computer for Britain's first digital aircraft, the Jaguar, and the world's first digital air data computer designed specifically for helicopters. The GEC Avionics Standard Central Air Data Computer is in service on some 5,000 US military aircraft. The company's range of video and data recording systems includes data loading systems for the Tornado IDS.

Smiths Industries' compact health and usage monitoring system provides constant information on temperature, overspeeds, engine starts and running hours. Its flight management system control and display units are in operation on the Airbus A-310, and the company is developing a new flight management system for Boeing 737s. Its standard flight data recorder is fitted to 17 US Air Force aircraft types.

THORN EMI Electronics specialises in harsh environment recorders and instrumentation recording systems for military purposes. Their reliability and compactness make them well suited for use in fighter aircraft and missiles. Racal produces a voice-logging recorder ideally suited for civil and military airfield installations.

Training Simulators and Systems

Britain's aerospace industry has played a major role in the development of flight simulators and trainers, which are more flexible and far less costly than airborne training. Like aircraft, simulators have become increasingly complex. British aircraft and ground control simulators are sold extensively overseas. Leading manufacturers include Rediffusion Simulation, Europe's largest simulator products manufacturer, Link-Miles, British Aerospace and Ferranti International.

Link-Miles developed the first ever fully microprocessor-based flight simulator using distributed processing, and the first computer-generated visual system based on microprocessors. It is unique in its experience of designing simulators for V/STOL combat aircraft. Its Harrier G5 simulator provides full training capability, with authentic avionics, weapons and sensor systems. Link-Miles has designed eight of the nine GR5 mission simulators for Harrier variants worldwide. Other recent programmes include simulators for the Boeing 747-400 and 737-300; the A129 combat mission helicopter; and the Sea Harrier Military Radar Trainer.

Rediffusion built Europe's first fully electronic simulator in 1950 for the Boeing Stratocruiser, having developed electronic navigation trainers during the second world war and the first flight simulators for jet fighters during the 1950s and 1960s. A winner of five Queen's Awards to Industry, it has pioneered many technological advances, including improved wide-angle visual displays and also touch-activated simulator control—the world's first simulator instructor facility to combine touch-screen computer graphics with microprocessor control. It has sold some 500 simulators and trainers worldwide.

Nowadays, all pilot conversion training and recurrent checks can be transferred from aircraft to simulators. The demands of 'zero flight time' training programmes and the training of crews to the most exacting of standards require a host of simulation technologies: accurate motion cues, realistic visuals, faithful reproduction of the aircraft's noises and instrumentation panels, and a fully integrated instructor console for flexible teaching.

Rediffusion's touch-activated simulator control decreases the instructor's workload and allows greater interaction with the crew. Its SP-X 'Novoview' range of systems generate a very high level of realism; its image generation systems are capable of simulating night-dusk or full daylight conditions. In display technology,

Rediffusion's projector-based WIDE system, in service for more than ten years, gives pilots a continuous, uninterrupted field-of-view. In 1990 the company launched Concept 90, which set new standards of simulator aesthetics, with enhanced ergonomic design.

Rediffusion has supplied around half of Britain's defence simulators and trainers. It devises and produces total training packages, from full flight simulators to low-cost simulators for smaller aircraft. British military aircraft supplied with Rediffusion simulators include the VC-10, Nimrod, Tornado GR1 and F3, and the Sea King helicopter. For the US Air Force, Rediffusion has provided simulation equipment for the B-52 bomber, E-3A AWACS (airborne warning and control system) and B-1 stealth bomber.

Virtual Reality

The most recent developments in training simulators are using the past decade's acceleration in computer technology to reproduce ever more realistic environments in a miniaturised and cost-saving way. Known as Virtual Reality (VR), this technology is being developed by British Aerospace through its Virtual Environment Configurable Training Aid (VECTA) system.

VR enables the pilot to see, through an optical view-finder, a three-dimensional reproduction of the cockpit and outside world, whether landscape, airfield or airborne. The 3-D effect is created by two miniature TV screens mounted in a flight helmet, positioned directly in front of the pilot's eyes. Each screen displays a slightly different view of the cockpit and 'outside world', giving a startling illusion of depth and perspective.

Airborne Communications Systems

Having pioneered many technical advances in airborne communications systems, the British electronics industry today produces civil and military transmitters and receivers across the entire frequency spectrum. It also builds telecommunication control systems for handling the distribution of radio signals to all forms of airborne navigation and communications systems.

The world's first UHF/VHF transceiver (combined transmitter and receiver) was designed by Plessey and is used widely. GEC Sensors, who pioneered the world's first use of radio in an aircraft, has employed its long experience in military ground-to-air communications technology to develop commercial systems. These include lightweight very high frequency (VHF) and ultra-high frequency (UHF) equipment for civil and military aircraft. It manufactures single and multiband radios and long-range communications systems for military and civil use, and offers an integration service in voice and data communications. The company's secure airborne communications systems enable strategic and intelligence information to pass between ground control and aircraft without the risk of interception. The GEC Sensors AD3500 system, which is highly resistant to jamming, is in use on the Harrier GR5. The company is involved in devising similar equipment for the European Fighter Aircraft. It has developed a total communications system for the EH101 helicopter.

Ferranti International is a world leader in the supply of systems for the aeronautical fixed telecommunications network (AFTN), a private international network operated by the world's national aviation authorities. The Ferranti AFTN switching system, being developed for the Belgian Airport and Airways Agency, supports a range of communications protocols, network services and connections. It will switch messages on the AFTN and other major global communications networks.

Lucas Aerospace has expanded into the commercial market for voice and data communications through the transfer of technologies from their military applications. Its ZS-1000 signal acquisition and direction finding system enables the pilot to acquire and sort signals on the basis of frequency and direction, giving a high degree of accuracy in conditions of poor signal reception.

Other communications equipment is produced by THORN EMI, Dowty, Racal, Marconi and British Aerospace.

Automatic Flight Control and Landing Systems

Modern flight control systems have advanced far beyond simple autopilot and flight path guidance systems. The growing adoption of fly-by-wire has had a fundamental effect on the performance and handling qualities of modern aircraft. This technology replaces traditional mechanical or cable-driven connections between the pilot's cockpit controls and the aircraft's control surfaces (actuators) with electronic systems. Dowty has been a pioneer here, and today produces fly-by-wire, fly-by-light and power-by-wire actuation systems for civil and military aircraft.

Concorde was the world's first civil airliner to use fly-by-wire, developed by GEC Avionics, as a primary means of control. A British Airways de Havilland Trident equipped with a British flight control system was the world's first commercial aircraft to be certificated to carry out automatic landings.

Fly-by-wire Systems
GEC Avionics is a world leader in 'fly-by-wire' with around 50 civil and military projects, having developed the automatic landing system for Concorde and advanced digital systems for Britain's Experimental Aircraft Programme.

The system enables the pilot's manipulation of the controls and rudder pedals to be passed directly to the aircraft's actuator control electronics (ACE), where the signals are digitised and sent to three primary flight computers. These assess the pilot's command signals and aircraft motion data to calculate the best configuration of the aircraft's control surfaces for optimum smooth flight in all conditions. Instructions are then passed back to the ACE. Each ACE manipulates the aircraft's primary and secondary control surfaces and returns drive commands to the pilot's controls.

GEC Avionics has been contracted to manufacture the fly-by-wire flight controls and primary computers for the Boeing 777, the first Boeing airliner to use the technology. GEC is also supplying spoiler control electronic units for the Canadair regional jet. These units command and monitor the aircraft's secondary flight control spoiler system governing lift during approach and landing.

A range of fly-by-wire equipment is built by GEC Avionics for military aircraft. For the European Fighter Aircraft, it is producing flight controls, flight-critical air data systems, and equipment for testing the performance of the utilities control system connecting the aircraft's fuel computers, flight control system, landing gear computers and generators. The company is also supplying flight controls for the US Advanced Tactical Fighter aircraft. GEC Avionics has also developed fly-by-light flight control systems.

Smiths Industries, which introduced the first all-electric British autopilot in 1947, has remained one of the world's leading manufacturers of all-weather flight control systems. Its work on the world's first fully automatic, certificated landing system for a passenger-carrying aircraft operating in poor visibility established the company's high reputation for advanced flight control systems. These were installed in the Trident fleets of British Airways, and a system was developed specifically for the RAF Jaguar. SI also introduced the first digital automatic flight control system for a passenger-carrying aircraft—the BAe 146.

With French and German partners, SI manufactures flight controls for the Airbus airliners, and 'smart' actuators for the Boeing 777's autothrottle control. Based on the company's experience with multi-axis stabilisation for helicopters, SI has also been selected, with Agusta of Italy, to build an automatic flight control system for the EH101 helicopter, which features a range of advanced autopilot functions.

Lucas Aerospace has remained at the leading edge of actuation technology ever since it provided the first powered flight control actuator for the stretched Caravelle over 30 years ago. Using electrical signalling to replace mechanical connections from pilot to actuator inputs was first adopted by Lucas in the early 1960s for the TSR-2. With the advent of high aircraft speeds, its powered actuators responded to the need to operate flying control surfaces against much higher aerodynamic loads.

Lucas went on to introduce advanced geared rotary, fly-by-wire servo and 'intelligent' actuators which incorporate digital electronic controls. The Airbus 320 is fitted with Lucas rotary actuators and all-electric signalled spoiler controls. An advanced Lucas fly-by-wire system is destined for the Apache helicopter. The company also makes missile fin control actuators.

Fairey Hydraulics is Europe's leading manufacturer of combat aircraft primary flight control actuator systems and is prime contractor for Harrier, Sea Harrier and Tornado. The compactness of its all-hydraulic rotary actuators makes them ideal for the very slim wings of agile combat aircraft. Fairey is making rotary direct drive valves for the European Fighter Aircraft's flight control system. A Fairey yaw auto-stabilisation system is in production for the BAe Hawk trainer/attack aircraft.

Fairey also produces thrust vector control actuation systems for rocket motors, and Decklock, a helicopter deck-landing system that gives maritime helicopters the ability to operate safely from the moving deck of a small ship. Orders for Decklock have been secured for the EH101, Westland Sea Kings for the Indian Navy, and Dolphin helicopters of the US Coast Guard.

Other Fairey control systems include a tail rotor actuator for the Lynx helicopter and a fin actuation system for the Spearfish torpedo. The company also makes fly-by-wire control systems for guided weapons.

Military Airborne Avionics

Although some of the equipment described above has been designed for dual civil and military purposes, the aerospace equipment industry manufactures systems specifically for military aircraft and missiles. Some companies are also involved in upgrading avionic systems on long-serving aircraft, enabling them to be retained and thereby saving costs. Smiths Industries, for example, has produced digital/solid state navigational and fuel gauging systems for updating the US Air Force's F-4.

Airborne Tactical Radars

A number of airborne tactical radars are in production in Britain. The first to go into service were made by Ferranti for the RAF Lightning and Buccaneer. Several companies manufacture thermal imaging and other electro-optical systems for aiming weapons and navigating by night.

The GEC Ferranti Foxhunter airborne interception radar for the Tornado F3 is designed to detect and track subsonic and supersonic targets at ranges in excess of 100 nautical miles. Its compact

Skyranger radar is intended for use in lightweight fighter aircraft. The company is developing multirole laser radars for fixed and rotary wing aircraft and missile guidance systems which can detect hazardous obstacles, such as wires and cables, at ranges greater than 2 km (1.24 miles). It also designs antennas for airborne radar systems in fast jet and rotary wing aircraft.

Airborne Surveillance Radars

THORN EMI Electronics has for many years made airborne surveillance radars for long-range maritime patrol aircraft. A notable example is the highly successful Searchwater radar installed in the Nimrod MR Mk 2. An airborne early warning version is in operation on Sea King helicopters. Searchwater provides maritime surveillance and tracking of all surface craft, with the ability to detect, track and classify simultaneously a large number of targets at long range. THORN EMI's demonstrator airborne stand-off radar is installed in the Pilatus Britten-Norman AEW Defender. It is designed to provide enhanced detection of moving ground targets.

GEC Ferranti's civil helicopter approach aid system provides safe, radar-guided, approaches to offshore objects, such as ships or platforms, in bad visibility. Its Seaspray 2000 maritime surveillance radar is used for detecting illegal fishing and smuggling in exclusive economic zones. Seaspray 3000 is installed in light naval helicopters, fixed wing aircraft and fast patrol boats for detection of surface targets for the Sea Skua anti-ship missile.

Thermal Imaging and Laser Systems

GEC Ferranti is the prime contractor for the Thermal Imaging and Television Airborne Laser Designator, an airborne laser targeting pod with infra-red and TV imaging for target acquisition and tracking. The system was in service with the RAF during the Gulf War in 1991 and was instrumental in destroying strategic targets. Currently being supplied for Tornado squadrons, it is suitable for a variety of aircraft.

GEC Ferranti's Thermal Surveillance System is fitted to RAF Puma helicopters. When coupled to a helmet tracking and display system, its Pilots Night Vision System, selected for the Italian Agusta 129 attack helicopter, enables pilots to see an image of the terrain in the direction they are looking.

Night Vision goggles enable pilots to perform low-flying operations by giving them the information needed to fly safely and effectively. The company has developed integrated helmets and helmet mounted displays for day and night operations.

Gunsights

Other weapon-aiming systems include gyroscopic gunsights, pioneered by GEC Ferranti and British Aerospace for use in Spitfires and Hurricanes during the second world war. GEC Ferranti's air-to-air ISIS gunsights are employed in light strike aircraft such as the Hawk. Its laser rangefinder, laser ranger and marked target seeker are operated with weapon-aiming computers and laser-guided munitions to ensure pinpoint accuracy in weapon delivery.

GEC Avionics, in conjunction with other European companies, is supplying weapon station units for the European Fighter Aircraft and weapons interface units for the RAF Tornado Mid Life Update programme. These systems act as the link for transferring high-frequency signals between the aircraft's subsystems and its weapon stations.

Surface Radars and Ground Systems

Perhaps the most important ground radar systems are used in air traffic control, where the growth in civilian air traffic requires increasingly sophisticated equipment to maintain safety standards. The industry also produces ground radar air defence systems incorporating electronic countermeasure features, as well as landing aids for use on airfields and ships and communications control systems for airports.

Microwave Landing Systems

The International Civil Aviation Organisation has approved a plan to replace instrument landing systems (ILS) by microwave landing systems (MLS). These have a number of advantages, including high resistance to interference reflected from the ground and nearby obstructions, and the ability to handle aircraft descending in a variety of approach paths over a wide range of angles. Siemens Plessey and Racal are active in this field.

Civil Radar Systems

Siemens Plessey manufactures radar systems for air traffic control, air defence, meteorology and naval and battlefield surveillance. It has supplied civil and military radar systems throughout the world for more than 35 years, including Britain's air defence network and civil air control system. The company's capability has been extended to supplying complete air traffic control systems.

Selected by the Civil Aviation Authority, the RAF and a large number of overseas customers, the Siemens Plessey Watchman civil air surveillance radar is in operation at Heathrow, Gatwick, Stansted, Manchester, Dubai and Bahrain airports. Incorporating the most advanced signal processing techniques to meet increasingly stringent user demands, Watchman offers exceptional coverage and high reliability in the most difficult ground and 'cluttered' weather environments.

The company's PLESSEX extractor/tracker filter system rejects 'angels' and false alarms while focusing on the detection of real targets. Although designed to work in conjunction with Watchman and the AR51 radar, PLESSEX can be used with other radars in a free-standing configuration.

Effective air traffic management is essential for handling a limited commodity such as airspace. Siemens Plessey's Controller air traffic management system, also used for air defence as the Commander (see p. 94), provides air traffic and associated data for air traffic controllers and airspace managers in a variety of situations, from small airports to large air traffic control centres.

With over 30 years' experience in the field, Racal has produced the Airfield Surface Movement Indicator (ASMI), in operation at many major airports; it was the first system to be installed at London Heathrow airport, in 1956. The ASMI gives enhanced performance in heavy weather clutter and can detail moving and stationary objects in all weather conditions. It can differentiate between all sizes of aircraft and will even detail a human figure at a 2 km (1.24 mile) range.

Cossor was one of the first firms in Britain to design and manufacture radar stations, that were to prove vital in the Battle of Britain in the second world war. It is now the main British producer of monopulse secondary surveillance radar for air traffic control. The Condor 9600 solid-state system, with high-definition displays, is in use with the Civil Aviation Authority, and more than 50 systems have been ordered by overseas civil aviation operators.

Military Radar Systems

Siemens Plessey is engaged in the implementation of the improved United Kingdom Air Defence System, having carried out the initial design studies. It is one of the world's leading suppliers of long-range three-dimensional radars, such as the AR-3D transportable air defence radar currently used in many countries. The AR-320, a NATO Class One long-range radar, was developed by Siemens Plessey and ITT of the United States for Britain's air defence.

The Siemens Plessey AR-325 Commander has been designed to meet the requirements of air defence forces worldwide. Commander's radar electronics are fully transportable in cabins by land, sea, and air, including helicopters and the C-130 aircraft. Its radars can be used in a basic track reporting post, or fully integrated with display and data handling facilities in more complex operation centres. Capable of detecting targets at a range of 470 km (250 miles), Commander is considered to be the most powerful transportable S band 3D radar available.

Siemens Plessey's Watchman radar system has its air defence equivalent, Tactical Watchman. The Guardsman 'C' system was designed for medium-range air and coastal defence, offering accurate tracking of fast, low-flying aircraft and helicopters. The radar electronics of this compact and highly mobile system are contained in a single cabin, which also houses the display and communications subsystems. The antenna mast can be elevated by a single operator.

The Multi-Function Electronic Scan Adaptive Radar (MESAR) demonstrator programme, jointly funded by the Defence Research Agency and Siemens Plessey, has been set up for the future manufacture of active array multifunction radars. MESAR is expected to be a lighter, more efficient radar than existing technology, and to be capable of detecting a large number of high-speed targets.

Marconi Radar Systems, Britain's largest ground radar manufacturer, is a long-established producer of air defence systems, including primary and secondary sensors, display systems and computers, secondary surveillance radars and electronic warfare systems. Its highly successful Martello long-range air defence system, developed for the RAF and in service worldwide, incorporates major advances in planar array, solid-state transmission and signal-processing technology. The S753 Tactical Transportable L band surveillance radar can maintain height cover of up to 30,000 m (100,000 ft) and a 'slant range' in excess of 200 nautical miles in severe weather and hostile electronic environments.

Identification Friend or Foe
Cossor Electronics provides an extensive range of Identification Friend or Foe (IFF) systems, which interrogate airborne movements on a radar screen. Since the mid-1950s, Cossor has developed and manufactured a variety of ground interrogators and airborne transponders. It produces the IFF 3500 interrogator for the RAF Tornado F3 air defence interceptor aircraft and supplies IFF for British weapons systems, such as Rapier.

Other Equipment

Aerial Targets and Remotely Piloted Vehicles
GEC Avionics is the prime contractor for Britain's battlefield remote surveillance system, Phoenix, with Flight Refuelling the main sub-contracting company for ground-based launch, recovery and command vehicles. Flight Refuelling's Advanced Subsonic

Aerial Target (ASAT) is a fully manoeuvrable, unmanned turbojet aircraft equipped to carry reconnaissance and electronic intelligence payloads.

Remotely piloted vehicles (RPVs) are made to serve as target systems for air-to-air and air-to-surface weapons training and are in service with air forces worldwide. They are also used by police and other authorities for surveillance and reconnaissance. Flight Refuelling has long experience in their production and has developed the Universal Drone Pack, a concise package of electronics enabling most types of manned aircraft to be operated unmanned, from take-off to landing. This allows them to be used for advanced training or missile development or in other roles too hazardous for manned operation.

Flight Refuelling's Raven is a multi-purpose RPV for tactical military and civil reconnaisance and is used as a training aid. It is navigated and controlled by a tracking radar and desk-top computer, or it can be controlled manually. Shorts makes the Skeet Mark 2 remote aerial target system for practice firing of close-range missiles and guns. It is in service with the British Army and overseas.

Landing Gear

Dowty Aerospace is a world leader in the field of undercarriages and their associated hydraulics. It is also Europe's largest manufacturer of aircraft landing gear, which has been fitted on over 200 military and civil aircraft types, including Tornado, Harrier, Sea Harrier, British Aerospace's EAP and BAe 146, and the Airbus A310, A320, A330 and A340 airliners.

AP Precision Hydraulics, which began designing hydraulically retractable undercarriages in the 1930s, produces landing gear for fixed wing commercial and military aircraft, including ship-borne fixed wing aircraft. Its ancillary products include steering gear, drag stays, door actuators, locks, and emergency hand pumps. The company is responsible for making the main landing gear for the BAe Hawk and the T-45A Goshawk, and for the EH101 helicopter.

Fairey Hydraulics manufactures its Deadlock landing gear range for light aircraft and helicopters such as the Islander, Trislander and Defender fixed wing aircraft, and the Westland 30 series and Lynx III helicopters. The latest landing gear is designed to absorb impacts at up to 6.1 metres (20 ft) per second without severe airframe damage or injury to occupants. The shock-absorbing element is made of advanced plastics. The Fairey nose landing gear for the Shorts Tucano is designed to accommodate increased G forces and descent velocities in a reduced space 'envelope'.

Brakes, Wheels and Tyres

Dunlop Aerospace Group, which includes an Aviation Division formed in 1925, is internationally renowned for a complete range of aircraft tyres, wheels, anti-skid and de-icing systems, carbon and steel brakes, and aircraft seals. Its lightweight carbon brakes, originally developed for Concorde, are standard equipment on many aircraft including, among others, the Boeing 757, BAe 146, ATP and EAP. More complex digital and analogue electronic braking systems include auto-braking during landing and rejected take-off. All braking systems give anti-skid protection.

Dunlop's range of crossply and radial tyres cover over 200 sizes in more than 300 configurations of speed, ply rating and tread depth. The 350 aircraft types fitted with Dunlop tyres include wide-body jets such as the A320, B747 and most commuter and military aircraft. With over 70 years' experience, the company uses the most advanced testing techniques to improve and expand its range to meet international requirements of durability and safety.

Seals

Dunlop manufactures airframe seals for all major European aircraft projects. Products range from polyurethane rain and dust erosion protection sheeting to inflatable seals for military aircraft. They comprise sound and pressure seals for doors, access hatches, passenger and pilot windows; aerodynamic seals on wing slats, flaps and control surfaces; and engine fire containment seals.

High-technology rubber components include silicone rubber seals for passenger doors. Seals made for Concorde completed 50,000 hours of testing before going into supersonic service; a similar design is used on passenger doors on the Fokker 100. The system consists of a main pressure seal on the outer edge of the door and a second seal on the inner edge, with a void between to create an acoustic barrier. A rubber vapour seal fitted to the BAe 146 ensures that the fuel vapour from the aircraft's central fuel tank is kept out of the passenger cabin.

Inflatable conductive rubber seals made by Dunlop for the Swedish Saab Gripen fighter aircraft keep the cockpit pressurised and prevent the intake of water. They also stop radio waves from interfering with the computerised controls.

De-icing and Fire Protection Systems

De-icing and anti-icing components are manufactured by Dunlop and Lucas Aerospace for aircraft leading edge surfaces, engine intakes, propellers and helicopter rotors. They incorporate electro-thermal heating elements with fibre-reinforced plastic structures and electronic control units to prevent overheating.

Kidde-Graviner has been a leading manufacturer of fire and overheat detection systems, fire extinguishers, smoke detectors and passenger oxygen systems for over 50 years. Its digital fire detection systems protect the engines of 150 civil and military fixed and rotary wing aircraft types. The company's continuous, automatically resetting detection system is designed to indicate fire or overheating in potentially hazardous areas, as well as local overheating and hot gas leaks from damaged de-icing and air-conditioning ducts. The detection system's status is monitored by the on-board maintenance computer, which can also detect short circuit failures and nacelle overheating.

On military aircraft, fuel tanks cover more than half the area prone to attack, with fuel fires and explosions causing over half of aircraft losses. Survivability systems made by Kidde-Graviner for military aircraft stem from the company's long experience in combustion and fire suppression technology.

For civil and military helicopters operating in adverse weather conditions and environments, rapidly acting systems to detect overheating and smoke and suppress fire are vital. Kidde-Graviner's specialised protection systems for helicopters include optical flame detectors and rapid discharge extinguishers for suppressing explosion fires; automatic flotation systems, liferafts and lifejacket inflators; and a switching system which activates the helicopter's fire protection systems in the event of a crash.

In-flight Refuelling Systems

The aviation pioneer Sir Alan Cobham first carried out experiments in air-to-air refuelling in 1934. His company, Flight Refuelling, introduced the 'probe-and-drogue' system of in-flight refuelling in 1949, and has since achieved a worldwide reputation for refuelling systems. It has supplied all the air-to-air refuelling equipment in service with the RAF and is making probe-and-drogue wing pods for a number of the US Air Force's strategic tanker fleet.

The company's latest refuelling pod is a self-contained store which enables a transport or bomber aircraft to convert to multi-point tanker. At sea, surface-to-air refuelling from ships adds a new dimension to the tactical capability of helicopters. Flight Refuelling's Ship-to-Helicopter system allows helicopters to be refuelled from ships that may not have a flight deck or whose flight deck is obstructed. The equipment is in service with the Royal Navy and several overseas navies.

Ejection Seats

Martin-Baker is the world's leading manufacturer of ejection seats and a pioneer in ejection seat technology. Over 6,000 lives have been saved by its seats, more than 65,000 of which have been delivered to 82 air forces. Having developed the first ejector seat in 1946 for a US Navy Douglas A-20 aircraft, the company continued to lead the field with the first ground-level live ejection demonstrations in Britain and the United States in 1955. All the US Navy's front line aircraft were subsequently retrofitted with Martin-Baker seats. The company's range is manufactured under licence in several overseas countries.

The Martin-Baker Mk.14 is the world's first electronically controlled ejection seat. Martin-Baker is developing the Navy Aircrew Ejection seat (NACES) for the US Navy, as well as other programmes for the Royal Navy, including the standard high-performance Navy safety seat. The Mk.16 is a high-performance escape system being tested for the EFA which is 30 per cent lighter than NACES and therefore also suitable for use in space vehicles within the Earth's atmosphere. The even lighter Mk.16L ejection seat is being devised for a range of training aircraft. Martin-Baker helicopter crashworthy seats have been selected for the Agusta A129 and EH101 helicopters.

Parachutes

The leading British supplier of parachutes to the Ministry of Defence is Irvin Great Britain. Irvin products are exported worldwide to civil and military customers. They range from parachute systems for aircrew, paratroops, supply dropping, free-fall and space-vehicle recovery, aircraft deceleration (brake 'chutes), and for the trajectory control of flares, sonobuoys, bombs and torpedoes. The company also manufactures aircraft passenger seat belts and aircrew lifejackets, life-preservers, anti-G clothing and harnesses.

Addresses

Department of Trade and Industry, Ashdown House, Victoria Street, London SW1H 0ET.

Ministry of Defence, Whitehall, London SW1A 3HB.

British National Space Centre, Dean Bradley House, 52 Horseferry Road, London SW1P 2AG.

Civil Aviation Authority, CAA House, 45–59 Kingsway, London WC2B 6TE.

British Aerospace Establishment, Farnborough, Hampshire GU14 6TD.

Society of British Aerospace Companies, 29 King Street, London SW1Y 6RD.

British Aerospace PLC, 11 The Strand, London WC2N 5HR.

Rolls-Royce PLC, 65 Buckingham Gate, London SW1E 6AT.

Westland Group PLC, Yeovil BA20 2YB.

Short Brothers PLC, PO Box 241, Airport Road, Belfast BT3 9D2.

Further Reading

Britain in Aerospace, Society of British Aerospace Companies, 29 King Street, St James's, London SW1Y 6RD.

Abbreviations

AMI	Active Microwave Instrument
ACE	Actuator control electronics
AMRAAM	Advanced medium-range air-to-air missile
ANR	Advanced non-rigid
ASRAAM	Advanced short-range air-to-air missile
ASAT	Advanced Subsonic Aerial Target
ATP	Advanced turboprop
AFTN	Aeronautical fixed telecommunications network
AWACS	Airborne warning and control system
ASMI	Airfield surface movement indicator
ADV	Air defence variant
ALARM	Air-launched anti-radar missile
ATSR	Along Track Scanning Radiometer
ASW	Anti-submarine warfare
BSE	Bristol-Siddeley Engines
BAe	British Aerospace
BAC	British Aircraft Corporation
BEA	British European Airways
BERP	British Experimental Rotor Programme
BHC	British Hovercraft Corporation
BNSC	British National Space Centre
BOAC	British Overseas Airways Corporation
CRT	Cathode-ray tube
CARAD	Civil Aircraft Research and Demonstration
CAA	Civil Aviation Authority
CIS	Commonwealth of Independent States
DRA	Defence Research Agency
DTI	Department of Trade and Industry
EODC	Earth Observation Data Centre
ECR	Electronic combat and reconnaissance
EMU	Engine monitoring unit
ECS	European Communications Satellite
EFA	European Fighter Aircraft
ERS	European Remote Sensing
ESA	European Space Agency
EAP	Experimental Aircraft Programme

FLIR	Forward Looking Infra Red
FADEC	Full-authority digital electronic control
GPS	Global Positioning System
HSA	Hawker-Siddeley Aviation
HUD	Head-up display
HUDWAC	Head-up display weapon-aiming computer
HMD	Helmet-mounted display
HOTOL	Horizontal take-off and landing
IFF	Identification Friend or Foe
ILS	Instrument landing systems
IDS	Interdictor strike
IAE	International Aero Engines
MLS	Microwave landing systems
MoD	Ministry of Defence
MESAR	Multi-Function Electronic Scan Adaptive Radar
MLRS	Multiple launch rocket system
NASA	National Aeronautics and Space Administration
NRSC	National Remote Sensing Centre
NACES	Navy Aircrew Ejection Seat
NOx	Nitrogen oxide
NGL	Normalair-Garrett
NATO	North Atlantic Treaty Organisation
RJ	Regional Jetliner
R & D	Research & development
RPV	Remotely piloted vehicle
RAE	Royal Aerospace Establishment
RAF	Royal Air Force
RN	Royal Navy
SERC	Science and Engineering Research Council
SI	Smiths Industries
SBAC	Society of British Aerospace Companies
SOHO	Solar Heliospheric Observatory
V/STOL	Vertical or short take-off and landing
VHF	Very high frequency
VOR	Very high frequency Omnirange
VECTA	Virtual Enrivonment Configurable Training Aid
VR	Virtual reality
UHF	Ultra-high frequency

Index

Fuel:
   consumption 11, 69
   gauges 81
   pump 72
   systems, 23

Gazelle helicopter 11, 49
GEC Avionics 19, 24, 77, 78, 79, 80,
   86, 87, 91, 95-6
GEC Ferranti 77, 80-1, 89-91
GEC-Plessey Avionics 24, 81-2
GEC Sensors 24, 76, 85
Germany 15, 25, 29, 40, 88
Giotto 58
Global Position System 60, 77
Gloster 4-5, 7
Goshawk 15, 24, 41, 97
Ground radar 91
Guardsmen *see* radar: military
Guided weapons 1, 23, 43-8
Gulf War 29, 91
Gunsights 91
Gyro compass instruments 77-8
Gyroscopes 78

Handley Page 10
   HP42 biplane 4
Harrier 2, 15, 23, 24, 38-9, 45, 70, 74,
   77, 80, 81, 83, 96
Hawk 15, 41-2, 70, 81, 88, 91, 97
Hawker 4
Hawker-Siddeley 12
Hawker-Siddeley Aviation (HSA) 5,
   15, 17, 18
'Head-up' display 2, 19, 79-81
Helicopters 15, 49-51, 71, 88
Helmet mounted display 80
Hipparcos 58
Hovercraft 2, 19, 52-3, 74
Hovermarine International 53
Hubble Space Telescope 58
Hughes Aircraft 25

Hunter 37
Hunting Engineering 48
Hunting Technical Services 64
Hurricane 5-6, 91

Identification Friend or Foe 95
IMI Summerfield 48
Imperial Airways 5
India 41, 77
Inertial navigation 77-8
In-flight refuelling 99-100
Inmarsat 60
Intelsat 59
International Aero Engines 65-6
International Civil Aviation
   Organisation 92
International Ultraviolet Explorer 58
Inter-war developments 4-6
Irvin Great Britain 101
Island Aircraft 22
   Islander/Defender 35, 43, 97
Italy 15, 25, 28

Jaguar 15, 25, 37, 65, 70, 77, 78, 80,
   82, 87
Japan 25, 58
JAS 39 Gripen 24-5
Javelin 47
Jet engines 7-8
Jet Provost 35
Jetstream *see* British Aerospace

Kestrel 5
Kidde-Graviner 48, 98-9

Lancaster 7
Landing gear 23, 96-7
Landsat 62
Leopard 35
Lifejacket 99
Link-Miles 24, 82-3
Lockheed 16, 18

Printed in the UK for HMSO.
Dd.0295921, 2/93, C30, 51-2423, 5673.

A MONTHLY UPDATE

ASPECTS OF BRITAIN

Current Affairs
a monthly survey

September 1992 Vol 22 No 9

London Conference on Former Yugoslavia
Outcome of the EC/UN Peace Conference

Balance of Payments 1991
Balance of Payments 'Pink Book'

Iraq
Deployment of Allied Military Aircraft over Southern Iraq

Research and Development
The Government's Annual Review of R & D

Regional Trends
Analysis of Regional Contrasts in Britain

CURRENT AFFAIRS:
A MONTHLY SURVEY

Using the latest authoritative information from official and other sources, *Current Affairs* is an invaluable digest of important developments in all areas of British affairs. Focusing on policy initiatives and other topical issues, its factual approach makes it the ideal companion for *Britain Handbook* and *Aspects of Britain*. Separate sections deal with governmental; international; economic; and social, cultural and environmental affairs. A further section provides details of recent documentary sources for these areas. There is also a twice-yearly index.

Annual subscription including index and postage £35·80 net.
Binder £4·95.

Buyers of Britain 1993: An Official Handbook *qualify for a discount of 25 per cent on a year's subscription to* Current Affairs *(see next page).*

HMSO Publications Centre
(Mail and telephone orders only)
PO Box 276
LONDON SW8 5DT
Telephone orders: 071 873 9090